STABILIZING SELF-DYNAMIC SOCIOECONOMIES
Evolutionary and ecological perspectives on farming economic systems for human needs

Rodrick Wallace
Division of Epidemiology
The New York State Psychiatric Institute
rodrick.wallace@gmail.com

November 26, 2011

Preface

The creation of economic institutions that can function well under the impact of substantial 'non quantifiable' risks is analogous to the dilemmas confronting our hunter-gatherer forefathers in the face of large-scale ecological uncertainties. The ultimate solution was not the development of a super hunter-gatherer technology that could ride out repeated catastrophe, but rather the invention, in neolithic times, of culturally-adapted 'farmed' ecosystems constructed so as to maximize food yield and minimize risks of famine.

Farmed, as opposed to hunter-gatherer, ecosystems permitted, in turn, a transition to village, city, and larger scale human communities. From that perspective, our current boom-and-bust 'globalized' economy might be seen as primitive indeed, and may not permit long-term maintenance of current levels of human population.

Recent advances in evolutionary and ecosystem theory applied to economic structure and process may permit construction of both new economic theory and new tools for data analysis that can help in the design of more robust economic institutions. This may result in less frequent and less disruptive Knightian transitions, and enable as well the design of culturally-specific systems less affected by those that do occur.

Generalized evolutionary theory has emerged as central to the description of economic process (e.g., Aldrich et al., 2008; Hodgson and Knudsen, 2010). Just as evolutionary principles provide necessary, but not sufficient, conditions for understanding the dynamics of social entities, so too the asymptotic limit theorems of information theory provide another set of necessary conditions that constrain socioeconomic evolution. These restrictions can be formulated as a statistics-like toolbox for the study of empirical data that is consistent with generalized evolutionary approaches, but escapes the intellectual straightjacket of replicator dynamics. The formalism is a coevolutionary theory in which punctuated convergence to temporary quasi-equilibria is inherently nonequilibrium, involving highly dynamic information sources – 'languages' – rather than system stable points.

From this perspective, the self-referential character of evolutionary process noted recently by Goldenfeld and Woese (2010), and by many others in the past, can be restated in the context of economic process through the language model. The underlying inherited and learned culture of the firm, the short-time cognitive response of the firm to patterns of threat and opportunity that is sculpted by that culture, and the embedding socioeconomic environment, can be represented as interacting information sources interfaced by artifacts of niche construction. If unregulated, the larger, compound, source that characterizes high probability evolutionary paths of this composite then becomes, literally, a self-dynamic language that speaks itself. Such a structure is indeed, for those enmeshed in it, more akin to a primitive hunter-gatherer society at the mercy of pathological internal dynamics than to a neolithic agricultural community in which an ordered, adapted, ecosystem is deliberately farmed so as to match its productivity to human needs.

All this being said, however, like 'ordinary' statistical inference, the theory presented here does not, by itself, do the science for us – the vain hope of mathematical equilibrium economics and analogous game theory approaches. Rather, the theory can provide a new set of tools for the empirical comparison of similar systems under different, and different systems under similar, observational (or experimental) conditions (e.g., D. Wallace and R. Wallace, 2000). And unlike dynamic game theory (e.g., Roca et al., 2009), the generalization to spatially, temporally, or socially structured systems, falls within standard (if difficult) analytic methodologies.

Chapter 1, based on Wallace (2011a), introduces the methodology, adapted from recent theoretical developments in evolutionary theory (Wallace, 2010; 2011b). The second chapter extends that perspective by restricting the formalism to examine the role of niche construction in fitness, a kind of lubrication between environmental demands and the 'phenotypic' responses possible to the firm. Chapter 3, based on Wallace (2011b), introduces explicit models related to the 'farming' of economic systems for maximal productivity and stability, and enumerates a spectrum of potential mathematical tools for data analysis. The mathematical demands vary, but most of the material should be accessible at the upper undergraduate level, with much tutorial material provided in chapter appendices.

A central and repeated feature of this work, however, is a cognitive paradigm linking 'replicator' and 'interactor' with the embedding environment, producing a complicated intermeshing that confounds simple compartmentalizations. For some, this will be a hard thing to digest.

New York City, November, 2011

References

Aldrich, R. G. Hodgson, D. Hull, T. Knudsen, J. Mokyr, V. Vanberg, 2008, In defense of generalized Darwinism, Journal of Evolutionary Economics, 18:577-596.

Goldenfeld, N., C. Woese, 2010, Life is physics: evolution as a collective phenomenon far from equilibrium, ArXiv:1011.4125v1 [q-bio.PE].

Hodgson, G, T. Knudsen, 2010, Darwin's Conjecture: The search for general principles of social and economic evolution, University of

Chicago Press.

Roca, C., J. Cuesta, A. Sanchez, 2009, Evolutionary game theory: temporal and spatial effects beyond replicator dynamics, Physics of Life Reviews, 6:208-249.

Wallace, D., R. Wallace, 2000, Life and death in Upper Manhattan and the Bronx: toward an evolutionary perspective on catastrophic social change, Environment and Planning A, 32:1245-1266.

Wallace, R., 2010, Expanding the Modern Synthesis, Comptes Rendus Biologies, 333:701-709.

Wallace, R., 2011a, A new formal approach to evolutionary processes in socioeconomic systems. In press, Journal of Evolutionary Econonmics, doi 10.1007/s00191-011-0237-1.

Wallace, R., 2011b, A formal approach to evolution as self-referential language, BioSystems, 106:36-44.

Contents

Chapter 1

Evolutionary economics

1.1 Introduction

Aldrich et al. (2008) make a compelling case that Darwinian principles cover the evolution of social or economic entities. They find that,
although there are important differences between biological and cultural domains and the selection processes that affect them, and the
particulars of Darwinian mechanisms of variation, inheritance, and selection differ in important ways, yet the overarching general principles
remain. They argue that we must regard institutions as cohesive entities having some capacity for the retention and replication of problem
solutions, and that innovation is about the creation of new variations,
while selection is about how these are tested in the real world. An
essential strain in their argument is a paradigm of program-based behavior that requires an explanation of emergence through both natural
selection and individual development, in the context of Eldredge and
Gould's 'punctuated equilibria' (Gould, 2002).

A more recent, broader scale, study by Hodgson and Knudsen
(2010) argues that

> Darwinism as such provides no single model or ax-
> iomatic system. Instead, it is a metatheoretical framework
> that stimulates further inquiry and provides a repository
> for contingent auxiliary theories and models... the con-
> struction of a new Darwinian theoretical system capable of
> generating powerful predictive models to rival established
> alternatives in the social sciences is a long way off. As
> with the application of Darwinian principles to biology,
> the first and principal achievement is to build a concep-
> tual engine that is capable of guiding specific inquiry into
> detailed causal mechanisms. The secondary process – of

showing how these principles operated in specific contexts
– required a century of detailed empirical and experimental study before Darwinism triumphed in the 1940's. The
task of applying Darwinism to the social sciences is much
younger and has far to go.

Here we will attempt to shorten this development period by introducing a series of necessary conditions statistical models based on the
asymptotic limit theorems of information theory that might well show
how these principles operate in specific empirical contexts.

The starting point is a recent expansion of the classic Modern Evolutionary Synthesis that takes into account the critical role of interaction in the real world (Wallace, 2010), a matter of current interest
in economics from dangerously simplistic perspectives (e.g., Johnson,
2011).

Lewontin (2010), reviewing the book by Fodor and Piatelli-Palmarini
(2010), describes the Modern Evolutionary Synthesis as having four
basic metaphorical principles:

(1) **The principle of variation:** Among individuals in a population there is variation in form, physiology, and behavior.

(2) **The principle of heredity:** Offspring resemble their parents
more than they resemble unrelated individuals.

(3) **The principle of differential reproduction:** In a given
environment, some forms are more likely to survive and produce more
offspring than other forms.

(4) **The principle of mutation:** New heritable variation is constantly occurring.

Lewontin, however, finds this structure lacking, in that "...there
is an immense amount of biology that is missing", largely involving
interactions within and across structures and entities at various scales.

To address this lack, Wallace (2010) introduces a fifth principle:

(5) **The principle of environmental interaction:** Individuals
and groups engage in powerful, often punctuated, dynamic mutual
relations with their embedding environments that may include the
exchange of heritage material between markedly different organisms.

Again, details surrounding the reasons for this introduction can be
found in Wallace, (2010).

The central innovation is to describe embedding ecosystem, genetic heritage, and (cognitive) gene expression in terms of interacting information sources whose dynamics are driven by the homology
between information source uncertainty and free energy density in a
series of regression-like relations similar to the empirical Onsager equations of nonequilibrium thermodynamics. Taking much the perspective of Champagnat et al. (2006), the resulting theory is inherently
coevolutionary, in the largest sense, so that there is no single 'natural'

scale at which 'selection' takes place. There is, rather, a set of interactive quasi-equilibria subject to often highly structured large deviations representing the punctuated equilibria of Eldredge and Gould (1972), as well as possibly larger, hierarchical, conformations.

Here we adapt these results to the program of Hodgson and Knudson (2010), and begin by restating some familiar phenomena as information sources, leading to a formal structure that expresses these extensions in terms of familiar coevolutionary models. See the Mathematical Appendix to this chapter for a brief summary of basic results from information theory.

1.2   Ecosystems as information sources

Firms interact with – and affect – embedding environments. Here we reexpress social and economic 'ecosystems' in terms of the rough regularities of their behavior, essentially a grammar and syntax, without demanding dynamic or stochastic simplicity: We characterize them as information sources – generalized languages – capable of structured output within broad constraints.

First consider a simplistic picture of a predator/prey ecosystem. Let X represent the appropriately scaled number of 'predators', Y the scaled number of 'prey', t the time, and ω a parameter defining their interaction. The model assumes that the ecologically dominant relation is an interaction between predator and prey, so that $dX/dt = \omega Y$ and $dY/dt = -\omega X$

Thus the predator populations grows proportionately to the prey population, and the prey declines proportionately to the predator population.

After differentiating the first and using the second equation, we obtain the simple relation $d^2X/dt^2 + \omega^2 X = 0$ having the solution $X(t) = sin(\omega t); Y(t) = cos(\omega t)$. Thus $X(t)^2 + Y(t)^2 = sin^2(\omega t) + cos^2(\omega t) \equiv 1$.

In the two dimensional phase space defined by $X(t)$ and $Y(t)$, the system traces out an endless, circular trajectory in time, representing the out-of-phase sinusoidal oscillations of the predator and prey populations.

Divide the $X - Y$ phase space into two components – the simplest coarse graining – calling the halfplane to the left of the vertical Y-axis A and that to the right B. This system, over units of the period $1/(2\pi\omega)$, traces out a stream of A's and B's having a single very precise grammar and syntax: $ABABABAB...$

Many other such statements might be conceivable, e.g.,

$AAAAA..., BBBBB..., AAABAAAB..., ABAABAAAB...,$

and so on, but, of the obviously infinite number of possibilities, only one is actually observed, is 'grammatical': $ABABABAB....$

More complex dynamical system models, incorporating diffusional drift around deterministic solutions, or even very elaborate systems of complicated stochastic differential equations, having various domains of attraction, that is, different sets of grammars, can be described by analogous symbolic dynamics (Beck and Schlogl, 1993, Ch. 3).

Rather than taking symbolic dynamics as a simplification of more exact analytic or stochastic approaches it is possible to generalize symbolic dynamics to a more comprehensive structure. Social, economic, or biological ecosystems may not have identifiable sets of stochastic dynamic equations like noisy, nonlinear mechanical clocks, but, under appropriate coarse-graining, they may still have recognizable sets of grammar and syntax over the long-term. The turn-of-the seasons in a temperate climate, for many natural communities, looks remarkably the same year after year: the ice melts, the migrating birds return, the trees bud, the grass grows, plants and animals reproduce, high summer arrives, the foliage turns, the birds leave, frost, snow, the rivers freeze, and so on. In a social setting, interacting actors can be expected to behave within fairly well defined cultural and historical constraints, depending on context: birthday party behaviors are not the same as cocktail party behaviors in a particular social set, but both will be characteristic.

Suppose it possible to coarse grain the ecosystem at time t according to some appropriate partition of the phase space in which each division A_j represent a particular range of numbers of each possible fundamental actor in the generalized ecosystem, along with associated larger system economic or other parameters. What is of particular interest is the set of longitudinal paths, that is, ecological or social system statements of the form $x(n) = A_0, A_1, ..., A_n$ defined in terms of some natural time unit of the system. Thus n corresponds to an again appropriate characteristic time unit T, so that $t = T, 2T, ..., nT$.

To reiterate, the central interest is in the *serial correlations along paths*.

Let $N(n)$ be the number of possible paths of length n that are consistent with the underlying grammar and syntax of the appropriately coarsegrained eco- or social system.

The fundamental assumptions are that – for this chosen coarsegraining – $N(n)$, the number of possible grammatical paths, is much smaller than the total number of paths possible, and that, in the limit of (relatively) large n,

$$H = \lim_{n \to \infty} \frac{\log[N(n)]}{n}$$

(1.1)

both exists and is independent of path.

This is a critical foundation to, and limitation on, the modeling strategy and its range of strict applicability, but is, in a sense, fairly general since it is *independent of the details of the serial correlations along a path.*

These conditions are the essence of the parallel with parametric statistics. Systems for which the assumptions are not true will require special nonparametric approaches. One is inclined to believe, however, that, as for parametric statistical inference, the methodology will prove robust in that many systems will sufficiently fulfill the essential criteria.

Nonetheless, not all possible ecosystem coarse-grainings are likely to work, and different such divisions, even when appropriate, might well lead to different descriptive quasi-languages for the ecosystem of interest. The example of Markov models is relevant. The essential Markov assumption is that the probability of a transition from one state at time T to another at time $T + \Delta T$ depends only on the state at T, and not at all on the history by which that state was reached. If changes within the interval of length ΔT are plastic, or path dependent, then attempts to model the system as a Markov process *within* the natural interval ΔT will fail, even though the model works quite well for phenomena separated by natural intervals.

Thus empirical identification of relevant coarse-grainings for which this body of theory will work is clearly not trivial, and may, in fact, constitute the hard scientific core of the matter.

This is not, however, a new difficulty in natural ecosystem theory. Holling (1992), for example, explores the linkage of ecosystems across scales, finding that mesoscale structures – what might correspond to the neighborhood in a human community – are ecological keystones in space, time, and population, and drive process and pattern at both smaller and larger scales and levels of organization.

In this spirit, Levin (1989) argues that there is no single correct scale of observation: the insights from any investigation are contingent on the choice of scales. Pattern is neither a property of the system alone nor of the observer, but of an interaction between them. Pattern exists at all levels and at all scales, and recognition of this multiplicity of scales is fundamental to describing and understanding ecosystems. In his view there can be no 'correct' level of aggregation: we must recognize explicitly the multiplicity of scales within ecosystems, and develop a perspective that looks across scales and that builds on a multiplicity of models rather than seeking the single 'correct' one.

Given an appropriately chosen coarse-graining, define joint and conditional probabilities for different ecosystem paths, having the form $P(A_0, A_1, ..., A_n)$, $P(A_n|A_0, ..., A_{n-1})$, such that appropriate joint and conditional Shannon uncertainties can be defined on them. For paths of length two these would be of the form

$$H(X_1, X_2) \equiv -\sum_j \sum_k P(A_j, A_k) \log[P(A_j, A_k)]$$

$$H(X_1|X_2) \equiv -\sum_j \sum_k P(A_j, A_k) \log[P(A_j|A_k)],$$

(1.2)

where the X_j represent the stochastic processes generating the respective paths of interest.

The essential content of the Shannon-McMillan Theorem is that, for a large class of systems characterized as information sources, a kind of law-of-large numbers exists in the limit of very long paths, so that

$$H[X] = \lim_{n \to \infty} \frac{\log[N(n)]}{n} =$$

$$\lim_{n \to \infty} H(X_n|X_0, ..., X_{n-1}) =$$

$$\lim_{n \to \infty} \frac{H(X_0, X_1, ..., X_n)}{n+1}.$$

(1.3)

Taking the definitions of Shannon uncertainties as above, and arguing backwards from the latter two equations (Khinchin, 1957), it is indeed possible to recover the first, and divide the set of all possible ecosystem temporal paths into two subsets, one very small, containing the grammatically correct, and hence highly probable paths, that we will call 'meaningful', and a much larger set of vanishingly low probability.

Basic material on information theory can be found in any number of texts, for example, Ash (1990), Khinchin (1957), Cover and Thomas (1991). A summary is given in the Mathematical Appendix to this chapter.

1.3 Corporate heritage

Adami et al. (2000) make a case for reinterpreting the Darwinian transmission of genetic heritage in terms of a formal information process: genomic complexity can be identified with the amount of information a sequence stores about its environment. Thus genetic complexity can be defined in a consistent information-theoretic manner. Most particularly, in their view, information cannot exist in a vacuum and must be instantiated. For biological systems information is instantiated, in part, by DNA. To some extent it is the blueprint of an organism and thus information about its own structure. More specifically, it is a blueprint of how to build an organism that can best survive in its native environment, and pass on that information to its progeny. Adami et al. assert that an organism's DNA thus is not only a 'book' about the organism, but also a book about the environment it lives in, including the species with which it co-evolves. They identify the complexity of genomes by the amount of information they encode about the world in which they have evolved.

Ofria et al. (2003) continue in the same direction and argue that genomic complexity can be defined rigorously within standard information theory as the information the genome of an organism contains about its environment. From the point of view of information theory, it is convenient to view Darwinian evolution on the molecular level as a collection of information transmission channels, subject to a number of constraints. In these channels, they state, the organism's genome codes for the information (a message) to be transmitted from progenitor to offspring, subject to noise from an imperfect replication process and multiple sources of contingency. Information theory is concerned with analyzing the properties of such channels, how much information can be transmitted and how the rate of perfect information transmission of such a channel can be maximized.

Adami and Cerf (2000) argue, using simple models of genetic structure, that the information content, or complexity, of a genomic string by itself (without referring to an environment) is a meaningless concept and a change in environment (catastrophic or otherwise) generally leads to a pathological reduction in complexity.

The transmission of genetic information is thus a contextual matter involving operation of an information source that, according to this perspective, must interact with embedding (ecosystem) structures.

The essential analogy, at the level of the firm, is that there will be a persistent, temporally transmitted, corporate culture, a transmitted backbone of learned habit, that, while modifiable in the long term, will strongly constrain short-term behaviors. We do not invoke replicator dynamics for the description of this corporate culture, but characterize it as another information source, a quasi-language, having recognizable grammar and syntax, so that certain kinds of behavioral 'statements' have high probability, and others are either impossible or highly improbable.

1.4 Cognitive behavior

A broad class of cognitive organizational phenomena – necessarily occurring on a relatively short timescale compared with the development and transmission of a corporate culture – can be characterized in terms of a dual information source that can interact with other such sources. The argument is straightforward. Atlan and Cohen (1998) argue that the essence of cognition is comparison of a perceived external signal with an internal, learned picture of the world, and then, upon that comparison, the choice of one response from a much larger repertoire of possible responses. Such reduction in uncertainty inherently carries information, and it is possible to make a very general model of this process as an information source (Wallace, 2005).

Cognitive pattern recognition-and-selected response, as conceived here, proceeds by convoluting an incoming external 'sensory' signal with an internal 'ongoing activity' – which includes, but is not limited to, a learned picture of the world – and, at some point, triggering an appropriate action based on a decision that the pattern of sensory activity requires a response. It is not necessary to specify how the pattern recognition system is trained, and hence possible to adopt a weak model, regardless of learning paradigm, that can itself be more formally described by the asymptotic limit theorems of information theory. Fulfilling Atlan and Cohen's (1998) criterion of meaning-from-response, it is possible to define a language's contextual meaning entirely in terms of system output.

The model is as follows.

A pattern of 'sensory' input, say an ordered sequence $y_0, y_1, ...,$ is mixed in a systematic (but unspecified) algorithmic manner with internal 'ongoing' activity, a sequence $w_0, w_1, ...,$ to create a path of composite signals $x = a_0, a_1, ..., a_n, ...,$ where $a_j = f(y_j, w_j)$ for some function f. This path is then fed into a highly nonlinear, but otherwise similarly unspecified, decision function generating an output $h(x)$ that is an element of one of two (presumably) disjoint sets B_0 and B_1. We take $B_0 \equiv \{b_0, ..., b_k\}, B_1 \equiv \{b_{k+1}, ..., b_m\}$.

Thus the structure permits a graded response, supposing that if $h(x) \in B_0$ the pattern is not recognized, and if $h(x) \in B_1$ the pattern is recognized and some action $b_j, k + 1 \leq j \leq m$ takes place.

The principal focus of interest is those composite paths x triggering the pattern recognition-and-response. That is, given a fixed initial state a_0, such that $h(a_0) \in B_0$, one examines all possible subsequent paths x beginning with a_0 and leading to the event $h(x) \in B_1$. Thus $h(a_0, ..., a_j) \in B_0$ for all $0 \leq j < m$, but $h(a_0, ..., a_m) \in B_1$.

For each positive integer n let $N(n)$ be the number of grammatical and syntactic high probability paths of length n which begin with some particular a_0 having $h(a_0) \in B_0$ and lead to the condition $h(x) \in B_1$. Call such paths meaningful and assume $N(n)$ to be considerably less than the number of all possible paths of length n – pattern recognition-and-response is comparatively rare. Again assume that the longitudinal finite limit $H \equiv \lim_{n \to \infty} \log[N(n)]/n$ both exists and is independent of the path x. Call such a cognitive process *ergodic*.

Disjoint partition of state space may be possible according to sets of states which can be connected by meaningful paths from a particular base point, leading to a natural coset algebra of the system, a groupoid. This is a matter of some importance pursued at length in Wallace et al. (2009).

It is thus possible to define an ergodic information source **X** associated with stochastic variates X_j having joint and conditional probabilities $P(a_0, ..., a_n)$ and $P(a_n | a_0, ..., a_{n-1})$ such that appropriate joint and conditional Shannon uncertainties may be defined which satisfy the relations above.

This information source is taken as *dual* to the ergodic cognitive process.

Again, the Shannon-McMillan Theorem and its variants provide 'laws of large numbers' permitting definition of the Shannon uncertainties in terms of cross-sectional sums of the form $H = - \sum P_k \log[P_k]$, where the P_k constitute a probability distribution.

Different quasi-languages will be defined by different divisions of the total universe of possible responses into various pairs of sets B_0 and B_1. Like the use of different distortion measures in the Rate Distortion Theorem, however, it seems obvious that the underlying dynamics will all be qualitatively similar.

Nonetheless, dividing the full set of possible responses into the sets B_0 and B_1 may itself require higher order cognitive decisions by another module or modules, suggesting the necessity of choice within a more or less broad set of possible quasi-languages. This would directly reflect the need to shift gears according to the different challenges faced by the organization or a subsystem. A critical problem then becomes the choice of a normal zero-mode language among a very large set of possible languages representing accessible excited states. This is a fundamental matter which mirrors, for isolated cognitive systems, the resilience arguments applicable to more conventional ecosystems, that is, the possibility of more than one zero state to a cognitive system. Identification of an excited state as the zero mode becomes, then, a kind of generalized autoimmune disorder that can be triggered by linkage with external ecological information sources that might represent various kinds of structured stress.

In sum, meaningful paths – creating an inherent grammar and syntax – have been defined entirely in terms of system response, as Atlan and Cohen (1998) propose, a formalism that can easily be applied to the stochastic neuron in a neural network (Wallace, 2005).

Ultimately, it becomes necessary to parameterize the information source uncertainty of the dual information source to a cognitive pattern recognition-and-response with respect to one or more variates, writing $H[\mathbf{K}]$, where $\mathbf{K} \equiv (K_1, ..., K_s)$ represents a vector in a parameter space. Let the vector $\mathbf{K}$ follow some path in time, that is, trace out a generalized line or surface $\mathbf{K}(t)$. We assume that the probabilities defining H, for the most part, closely track changes in $\mathbf{K}(t)$, so that along a particular piece of a path in parameter space the information source remains as close to stationary – the probabilities are fixed in time – and ergodic as is needed for the mathematics to work. Such a system is characterized as 'adiabatic' in the physics literature. Between pieces it is possible to impose phase transition characterized by a renormalization symmetry, as done in Chapter 3 of Wallace et al. (2009). Such an information source will be termed 'adiabatically piecewise stationary ergodic' (APSE).

Again, the ergodic nature of the information sources is a generalization of the law of large numbers and implies that the long-time averages we will need to calculate can, in fact, be closely approximated by averages across the probability spaces of those sources. For nonergodic information sources, a function, $\mathcal{J}(x_n)$, of each path $x_n \to x$, may be defined, such that $\lim_{n \to \infty} \mathcal{J}(x_n) = \mathcal{J}(x)$, but $\mathcal{J}$ will not in general be given by the simple cross-sectional laws-of-large numbers analogs above (Khinchin, 1957). More details are given in Wallace et al. (2009).

The essential argument is that the long-term corporate heritage information source that changes slowly with experience or diffusion is the 'genotype' that constrains the cognitive behavior of the firm in the context of rapidly changing patterns of threat and opportunity. That is, the cognitive behavior of the firm is the 'phenotype', and selection, as is well known, acts on phenotypes.

1.5 Interacting sources

Here the three basic interacting information sources – embedding socioeconomic environment, slowly-changing corporate heritage, and rapid cognitive organizational response – are modeled using a formalism similar to that invoked both for nonequilibrium thermodynamics and traditional coevolution (e.g., Diekmann and Law, 1996).

Consider a set of information sources representing these three phenomena.

Use inverse measures $\mathcal{H}_j \equiv 1/H_j, j \neq m$ *as parameters for each of the others,* writing $H_m = H_m(K_1...K_s, ...\mathcal{H}_j...), j \neq m$, where the K_s represent other relevant parameters.

Now segregate the $\mathcal{H}_j$ according to their relative rates of change. Cognitive process would be among the most rapid, followed by ecosystem dynamics and corporate heritage.

The dynamics of such a system becomes a recursive network of stochastic differential equations, similar to those used to study many other highly parallel dynamic structures (Wymer, 1997).

Letting the K_j and $\mathcal{H}_m$ all be represented as parameters Q_j, (with the caveat that H_m not depend on $\mathcal{H}_m$), one can define a 'disorder' measure analogous to entropy in nonequilibrium thermodynamics, following the arguments of Wallace and Wallace (2008, 2009) and Wallace et al. (2009), $S_H^m \equiv H_m - \sum_i Q_i \partial H_m / \partial Q_i$ to obtain a complicated recursive system of phenomenological 'Onsager relations' stochastic differential equations,

$$dQ_t^j = \sum_i [L_{j,i}(t, ...\partial S_H^m/\partial Q^i ...)dt + \sigma_{j,i}(t, ...\partial S_H^m/\partial Q^i ...)dB_t^i]$$

$$= L_j(Q^1, ..., Q^n)dt + \sum_i \sigma(t, Q^1, ..., Q^n)dB_t^i,$$

(1.4)

where terms have been collected and expressed both the $\mathcal{H}$'s and the external K's in terms of the same Q_j.

The index m ranges over the crosstalk and it is possible to allow different kinds of 'noise' dB_t^i, having particular forms of quadratic variation that may, in fact, represent a projection of environmental factors under something like a rate distortion manifold (Glazebrook and Wallace, 2009).

One approach to this result hinges on the homology between information source uncertainty and free energy density, following the example of Feynman (2000). Then the S^m are analogous to entropies in nonequilibrium thermodynamics, and equation (1.4) is simply an empirical Onsager equation in the gradient of the entropies, recognizing that there are no 'reciprocal Onsager relations' possible for this system, since there is not local reversibility. For example the sequence ' eth ' does not have the same probability as ' the ' in English.

The basis of the general argument lies in the formal similarity between the expression for free energy density and information source uncertainty, explored in more detail in Wallace and Wallace (2008, 2009):

Let $F(K)$ be the free energy density of a physical system, K the normalized temperature, V the volume and $Z(K, V)$ the partition function defined from the Hamiltonian characterizing energy states E_i. Then

$$Z(V, K) = \sum_i \exp[-E_i(V)/K],$$

and

$$F(K) = \lim_{V \to \infty} -K \frac{\log[Z(V, K))}{V} \equiv \frac{\log[\hat{Z}(K, V)]}{V},$$

similar to the first part of equation (1.3).

If a nonequilibrium physical system is parameterized by a set of variables $\{Q_i\}$, then the empirical Onsager equations are defined in terms of the gradient of the entropy $S \equiv F - \sum_j Q_j dF/dQ_j$ as

$$dQ_j/dt = \sum_i L_{i,j} \partial S/\partial Q_i,$$

where the $L_{i,j}$ are empirical constants. The stochastic version is just equation (1.4), with 'S' defined in terms of information as

$$S_H^m \equiv H_m - \sum_i Q_i \partial H_m/\partial Q_i.$$

There are several obvious possible dynamic patterns:

1. Setting equation (1.4) equal to zero and solving for stationary points gives attractor states since the noise terms preclude unstable equilibria.

2. This system may converge to limit cycle or pseudorandom 'strange attractor' behaviors in which the system seems to chase its tail endlessly within a limited venue – the traditional Red Queen.

3. What is converged to in both cases is not a simple state or limit cycle of states. Rather it is an equivalence class, or set of them, of highly dynamic information sources coupled by mutual interaction through crosstalk. Thus 'stability' in this structure represents particular patterns of ongoing dynamics rather than some identifiable static configuration.

Here we are indeed deeply enmeshed in a highly recursive phenomenological stochastic differential equations (e.g., Zhu et al. 2007), but in a dynamic rather than static manner. The objects of this dynamical system are equivalence classes of information sources, rather than simple 'stationary states' of a dynamical or reactive chemical system. The necessary conditions of the asymptotic limit theorems of communication theory have beaten the mathematical thicket back one layer.

It is of some interest to compare these results to those of Diekmann and Law (1996), who invoke evolutionary game dynamics to obtain a first order canonical equation for coevolutionary systems having the form

$$ds_i/dt = K_i(s)\partial W_i(s'_i, s)|_{s'_i=s_i}.$$

(1.5)

The s_i, with $i = 1, ..., N$ denote adaptive trait values in a community comprising N species. The $W_i(s'_i, s)$ are measures of fitness of individuals with trait values s'_i in the environment determined by the resident trait values s, and the $K_i(s)$ are non-negative coefficients, possibly distinct for each species, that scale the rate of evolutionary change. Adaptive dynamics of this kind have frequently been postulated, based either on the notion of a hill-climbing process on an adaptive landscape or some other sort of plausibility argument.

When this equation is set equal to zero, so there is no time dependence, one obtains what are characterized as 'evolutionary singularities' or stationary points.

Diekmann and Law contend that their formal derivation of this equation satisfies four critical requirements:

1. The evolutionary process needs to be considered in a coevolutionary context.

2. A proper mathematical theory of evolution should be dynamical.

3. The coevolutionary dynamics ought to be underpinned by a microscopic theory.

4. The evolutionary process has important stochastic elements.

Equation (1.4) above is similar, although reached by a much different route, one giving elaborate patterns of phase transition punctuation in a highly natural manner (Wallace et al., 2009). Champagnat et al. (2006), in fact, derive a higher order canonical approximation extending equation (1.5) that is closer to equation (1.4), that is, a stochastic differential equation describing evolutionary dynamics. Champagnat et al. (2006) go even further, using a large deviations argument to analyze dynamical coevolutionary paths, not merely evolutionary singularities. They contend that in general, the issue of evolutionary dynamics drifting away from trajectories predicted by the canonical equation can be investigated by considering the asymptotic of the probability of 'rare events' for the sample paths of the diffusion.

By 'rare events' they mean diffusion paths drifting far away from the canonical equation. The probability of such rare events is governed by a large deviation principle: when a critical parameter (designated ϵ) goes to zero, the probability that the sample path of the diffusion is close to a given rare path ϕ decreases exponentially to 0 with rate $\mathcal{I}(\phi)$, where the 'rate function' $\mathcal{I}$ can be expressed in terms of the parameters of the diffusion. This result, in their view, can be used to study long-time behavior of the diffusion process when there are multiple attractive evolutionary singularities. Under proper conditions the most likely path followed by the diffusion when exiting a basin of attraction is the one minimizing the rate function I over all the appropriate trajectories. The time needed to exit the basin is of the order $\exp(H/\epsilon)$ where H is a quasi-potential representing the minimum of the rate function $\mathcal{I}$ over all possible trajectories.

An essential fact of large deviations theory is that the rate function $\mathcal{I}$ which Champagnat et al. (2006) invoke can almost always be expressed as a kind of entropy, that is, in the form $\mathcal{I} = -\sum_j P_j \log(P_j)$ for some probability distribution. This result goes under a number of names; Sanov's Theorem, Cramer's Theorem, the Gartner-Ellis Theorem, the Shannon-McMillan Theorem, and so forth (Dembo and Zeitouni, 1998). A more detailed exploration will take place in Chapter 3 below.

These considerations lead very much in the direction of equation (1.4) above, now seen as subject to internally-driven large deviations that are themselves described in terms of information sources providing another $\mathcal{H}$ parameter that can trigger punctuated shifts between quasi-stable modes, in addition to resilience transitions driven by 'catastrophic' external events that may well include the exchange of heritage information between different classes of organization or at different organizational scales.

Equation (1.4) provides a very general statistical model indeed.

1.6 Punctuated change

The model reexpresses external socioeconomic ecosystem dynamics, corporate cultural heritage, and corporate cognitive behavior generating 'behavioral phenotypes', in terms of interacting information sources. This instantiates Principle (5) of the Introduction, producing a system of stochastic differential equations closely analogous to those used to describe more traditional coevolutionary biological phenomena, and subject to punctuated resilience shifts driven by internal large deviations or by external perturbations.

We have used the formalism of an expanded Modern Synthesis (Wallace, 2010) to characterize something of a generalized Darwinism appropriate to the study of economic pattern and process, generating, in equation (1.4), what amount to dynamic regression models that can be fitted to real data. Like simple static regression models, these empirical Onsager equations can be used to compare behaviors of a single system under different, or different systems under the same, conditions. Like simple regression models, these do not do the hard business of scientific inference: the asymptotic limit theorems of probability theory, from the Central Limit to the Rate Distortion Theorem provide necessary, but not sufficient, structure.

Socioeconomic environments affect firms, and firms affect embedding environments. Organizations can, locally, engage in niche construction to protect themselves from environmental vagaries. Thus environments select phenotypes that, in a sense, select environments. Corporate culture records the result, as does the embedding socioeconomic landscape, and the system coevolves as a unit, with sudden, complicated transitions between the quasi-equilibria of equation (1.4).

This is a slightly different picture than envisioned by Aldrich et al. (2008) or by Hodgson and Knudsen (2010), but one that is, perhaps, more consonant with evolving evolutionary theory.

In contrast with Haldane and May (2011), and in agreement with Johnson (2011), we do not see simple models as providing a basis for policy decisions. Generalized Darwinism, and the related statistical models developed here, provide necessary conditions for many social system behaviors, but the hard work of science lies in using these constraints to analyze data, and proper data analysis alone, in an ideal world, supplies the primary rational basis for policy decisions. Mathematical models of complex ecosystem phenomena, in the sense of Pielou (1977, p.106), serve only to suggest directions for that analysis.

Most centrally, a cognitive paradigm for 'gene expression', in the largest sense, implies there is no deterministic 'mapping' as such between genotype and phenotype. Thus the distinction between them dissolves into a complex regulatory system profoundly affected by signals from the embedding world which that system, in turn, affects through a kind of niche construction. Again, see the Wallace (2010) for further discussion.

The next chapter restricts the general theory so as to examine the relation between niche construction, in the sense of Odling-Smee et al. (2003), and a measure of fitness in the disjunction between the phenotype of the firm and the demands of the embedding economic environment.

1.7   Mathematical Appendix

1.7.1   The Shannon Coding Theorem

Messages from a source, seen as symbols x_j from some alphabet, each having probabilities P_j associated with a random variable X, are 'encoded' into the language of a 'transmission channel', a random variable Y with symbols y_k, having probabilities P_k, possibly with error. Someone receiving the symbol y_k then retranslates it (without error) into some x_k, which may or may not be the same as the x_j that was sent.

More formally, the message sent along the channel is characterized by a random variable X having the distribution

$$P(X = x_j) = P_j, j = 1, ..., M.$$

The channel through which the message is sent is characterized by a second random variable Y having the distribution

$$P(Y = y_k) = P_k, k = 1, ..., L.$$

Let the joint probability distribution of X and Y be defined as

$$P(X = x_j, Y = y_k) = P(x_j, y_k) = P_{j,k}$$

and the conditional probability of Y given X as

$$P(Y = y_k | X = x_j) = P(y_k | x_j).$$

Then the Shannon uncertainty of X and Y independently and the joint uncertainty of X and Y together are defined respectively as

$$H(X) = -\sum_{j=1}^{M} P_j \log(P_j)$$

$$H(Y) = -\sum_{k=1}^{L} P_k \log(P_k)$$

$$H(X,Y) = -\sum_{j=1}^{M}\sum_{k=1}^{L} P_{j,k} \log(P_{j,k}).$$

(1.6)

The *conditional uncertainty* of Y given X is defined as

$$H(Y|X) = -\sum_{j=1}^{M}\sum_{k=1}^{L} P_{j,k} \log[P(y_k|x_j)]$$

(1.7)

For any two stochastic variates X and Y, $H(Y) \geq H(Y|X)$, as knowledge of X generally gives some knowledge of Y. Equality occurs only in the case of stochastic independence.

Since $P(x_j, y_k) = P(x_j)P(y_k|x_j)$, we have

$$H(X|Y) = H(X,Y) - H(Y)$$

The information transmitted by translating the variable X into the channel transmission variable Y – possibly with error – and then retranslating without error the transmitted Y back into X is defined as

$$I(X|Y) \equiv H(X) - H(X|Y) = H(X) + H(Y) - H(X,Y)$$

(1.8)

See, for example, Ash (1990), Khinchin (1957) or Cover and Thomas (1991) for details. The essential point is that if there is no uncertainty in X given the channel Y, then there is no loss of information through transmission.

In general this will not be true, and herein lies the essence of the theory.

Given a fixed vocabulary for the transmitted variable X, and a fixed vocabulary and probability distribution for the channel Y, we may vary the probability distribution of X in such a way as to maximize the information sent. The capacity of the channel is defined as

$$C \equiv \max_{P(X)} I(X|Y)$$

(1.9)

subject to the subsidiary condition that $\sum P(X) = 1$.

The critical trick of the Shannon Coding Theorem for sending a message with arbitrarily small error along the channel Y at any rate $R < C$ is to encode it in longer and longer 'typical' sequences of the variable X; that is, those sequences whose distribution of symbols approximates the probability distribution $P(X)$ above which maximizes C.

If $S(n)$ is the number of such 'typical' sequences of length n, then

$$\log[S(n)] \approx nH(X)$$

where $H(X)$ is the uncertainty of the stochastic variable defined above. Some consideration shows that $S(n)$ is much less than the total number of possible messages of length n. Thus, as $n \to \infty$, only a vanishingly small fraction of all possible messages is meaningful in this sense. This observation, after some considerable development, is what allows the Coding Theorem to work so well. In sum, the prescription is to encode messages in typical sequences, which are sent at very nearly the capacity of the channel. As the encoded messages become longer and longer, their maximum possible rate of transmission without error approaches channel capacity as a limit. Again, Ash (1990), Khinchin (1957) and Cover and Thomas (1991) provide details.

1.7.2 The 'tuning theorem'

Telephone lines, optical wave guides and the tenuous plasma through which a planetary probe transmits data to earth may all be viewed in traditional information-theoretic terms as a *noisy channel* around which we must structure a message so as to attain an optimal error-free transmission rate.

Telephone lines, wave guides and interplanetary plasmas are, relatively speaking, fixed on the timescale of most messages, as are most sociogeographic networks. Indeed, the capacity of a channel, according to equation 1.9, is defined by varying the probability distribution of the 'message' process X so as to maximize $I(X|Y)$.

Suppose there is some message X so critical that its probability distribution must remain fixed. The trick is to fix the distribution $P(x)$ but *modify the channel* – i.e. tune it – so as to maximize $I(X|Y)$. The *dual* channel capacity C^* can be defined as

$$C^* \equiv \max_{P(Y),P(Y|X)} I(X|Y)$$

(1.10)

But

$$C^* = \max_{P(Y),P(Y|X)} I(Y|X)$$

since

$$I(X|Y) = H(X) + H(Y) - H(X,Y) = I(Y|X).$$

Thus, in a purely formal mathematical sense, *the message transmits the channel*, and there will indeed be, according to the Coding Theorem, a channel distribution $P(Y)$ which maximizes C^*.

One may do better than this, however, by modifying the channel matrix $P(Y|X)$. Since

$$P(y_j) = \sum_{i=1}^{M} P(x_i)P(y_j|x_i),$$

$P(Y)$ is entirely defined by the channel matrix $P(Y|X)$ for fixed $P(X)$ and

$$C^* = \max_{P(Y),P(Y|X)} I(Y|X) = \max_{P(Y|X)} I(Y|X).$$

Calculating C^* requires maximizing the complicated expression

$$I(X|Y) = H(X) + H(Y) - H(X,Y)$$

which contains products of terms and their logs, subject to constraints that the sums of probabilities are 1 and each probability is itself between 0 and 1. Maximization is done by varying the channel matrix terms $P(y_j|x_i)$ within the constraints. This is a difficult problem in nonlinear optimization requiring Lagrange multiplier methods. However, for the special case $M = L$, C^* may be found by inspection: If $M = L$, then choose

$$P(y_j|x_i) = \delta_{j,i}$$

where $\delta_{i,j}$ is 1 if $i = j$ and 0 otherwise. For this special case

$$C^* \equiv H(X)$$

with $P(y_k) = P(x_k)$ for all k. *Information is thus transmitted without error when the channel becomes 'typical' with respect to the fixed message distribution $P(X)$.*

If $M < L$ matters reduce to this case, but for $L < M$ information must be lost, leading to Rate Distortion arguments explored more fully below.

Thus modifying the channel may be a far more efficient means of ensuring transmission of an important message than encoding that message in a 'natural' language which maximizes the rate of transmission of information on a fixed channel.

We have examined the two limits in which either the distributions of $P(Y)$ or of $P(X)$ are kept fixed. The first provides the usual Shannon Coding Theorem, and the second, hopefully, a tuning theorem variant. It seems likely, however, than for many important systems $P(X)$ and $P(Y)$ will 'interpenetrate,' to use Richard Levins' terminology. That is, $P(X)$ and $P(Y)$ will affect each other in characteristic ways, so that some form of mutual tuning may be the most effective strategy.

1.7.3 The Shannon-McMillan Theorem

Not all statements – sequences of the random variable X – are equivalent. According to the structure of the underlying language of which the message is a particular expression, some messages are more 'meaningful' than others, that is, in accord with the grammar and syntax of the language. The other principal result from information theory, the Shannon-McMillan or Asymptotic Equipartition Theorem, describes how messages themselves are to be classified.

Suppose a long sequence of symbols is chosen, using the output of the random variable X above, so that an output sequence of length n, with the form

$$x_n = (\alpha_0, \alpha_1, ..., \alpha_{n-1})$$

has joint and conditional probabilities

$$P(X_0 = \alpha_0, X_1 = \alpha_1, ..., X_{n-1} = \alpha_{n-1})$$

$$P(X_n = \alpha_n | X_0 = \alpha_0, ..., X_{n-1} = \alpha_{n-1}).$$

(1.11)

Using these probabilities we may calculate the conditional uncertainty

$$H(X_n | X_0, X_1, ..., X_{n-1}).$$

The uncertainty of the *information source*, $H[\mathbf{X}]$, is defined as

$$H[\mathbf{X}] \equiv \lim_{n \to \infty} H(X_n | X_0, X_1, ..., X_{n-1}).$$

(1.12)

In general

$$H(X_n | X_0, X_1, ..., X_{n-1}) \leq H(X_n).$$

Only if the random variables X_j are all stochastically independent does equality hold. If there is a maximum n such that, for all $m > 0$

$$H(X_{n+m} | X_0, ..., X_{n+m-1}) = H(X_n | X_0, ..., X_{n-1}),$$

then the source is said to be of *order* n. It is easy to show that

$$H[\mathbf{X}] = \lim_{n \to \infty} \frac{H(X_0, ... X_n)}{n+1}.$$

In general the outputs of the $X_j, j = 0, 1, ..., n$ are *dependent*. That is, the output of the communication process at step n depends on previous steps. Such serial correlation, in fact, is the very structure which enables most of what follows in this book.

Here, however, the processes are all assumed fixed, that is, the serial correlations do not change in time, and the system is *stationary*.

A very broad class of such self-correlated, stationary, information sources, the so-called *ergodic* sources for which the long-run relative frequency of a sequence converges stochastically to the probability assigned to it, have a particularly interesting property:

It is possible, in the limit of large n, to divide all sequences of outputs of an ergodic information source into two distinct sets, S_1 and S_2, having, respectively, very high and very low probabilities of occurrence, with the source uncertainty providing the splitting criterion. In particular the Shannon-McMillan Theorem states that, for a (long) sequence having n (serially correlated) elements, the number of 'meaningful' sequences, $N(n)$ – those belonging to set S_1 – will satisfy the relation

$$\frac{\log[N(n)]}{n} \approx H[\mathbf{X}].$$

(1.13)

More formally,

$$\lim_{n \to \infty} \frac{\log[N(n)]}{n} = H[\mathbf{X}]$$

$$= \lim_{n \to \infty} H(X_n | X_0, ..., X_{n-1})$$

$$= \lim_{n \to \infty} \frac{H(X_0, ..., X_n)}{n+1}.$$

(1.14)

The Shannon Coding theorem, by means of an analogous splitting argument, shows that for any rate $R < C$, where C is the channel capacity, a message may be sent without error, using the probability distribution for X which maximizes $I(X|Y)$ as the coding scheme. Using the internal structures of the information source permits *limiting attention only to meaningful sequences of symbols*. This restriction can greatly raise the maximum possible rate at which information can be transmitted with arbitrarily small error: if there are M possible symbols and the uncertainty of the source is $H[\mathbf{X}]$, then the effective capacity of the channel C, using this 'source coding,' becomes (Ash, 1990)

$$C_E = C \frac{\log(M)}{H[\mathbf{X}]}.$$

(1.15)

As $H[\mathbf{X}] \leq \log(M)$, with equality only for stochastically independent, uniformly distributed random variables,

$$C_E \geq C.$$

(1.16)

Note that, for a given channel capacity, the condition

$$H[\mathbf{X}] \leq C$$

always holds.

1.7.4 The Rate Distortion Theorem

The Shannon-McMillan Theorem can be expressed as the 'zero error limit' of the Rate Distortion Theorem (Dembo and Zeitouni, 1998; Cover and Thomas, 1991). The theorem defines a splitting criterion that identifies high probability pairs of sequences. We follow closely the treatment of Cover and Thomas (1991).

The origin of the problem is the question of representing one information source by a simpler one in such a way that the least information is lost. For example we might have a continuous variate between 0 and 100, and wish to represent it in terms of a small set of integers in a way that minimizes the inevitable distortion that process creates. Typically, for example, an analog audio signal will be replaced by a 'digital' one. The problem is to do this in a way which least distorts the *reconstructed* audio waveform.

Suppose the original stationary, ergodic information source Y with output from a particular alphabet generates sequences of the form

$$y^n = y_1, ..., y_n.$$

These are 'digitized,' in some sense, producing a chain of 'digitized values'

$$b^n = b_1, ..., b_n,$$

where the b-alphabet is much more restricted than the y-alphabet.

b^n is, in turn, *deterministically retranslated* into a reproduction of the original signal y^n. That is, each b^m is mapped on to a unique n-length y-sequence in the alphabet of the information source Y:

$$b^m \rightarrow \hat{y}^n = \hat{y}_1, ..., \hat{y}_n.$$

Note, however, that many y^n sequences may be mapped onto the *same* retranslation sequence $\hat{y}^n$, so that information will, in general, be lost.

The central problem is to explicitly minimize that loss.

The retranslation process defines a new stationary, ergodic information source, $\hat{Y}$.

The next step is to define a *distortion measure*, $d(y, \hat{y})$, which compares the original to the retranslated path. For example the *Hamming distortion* is

$$d(y, \hat{y}) = 1, y \neq \hat{y}$$

$$d(y, \hat{y}) = 0, y = \hat{y}.$$

(1.17)

For continuous variates the *Squared error distortion* is

$$d(y, \hat{y}) = (y - \hat{y})^2.$$

(1.18)

Possibilities abound.
The distortion between paths y^n and $\hat{y}^n$ is defined as

$$d(y^n, \hat{y}^n) = \frac{1}{n} \sum_{j=1}^{n} d(y_j, \hat{y}_j).$$

(1.19)

Suppose that with each path y^n and b^n-path retranslation into the y-language and denoted y^n, there are associated individual, joint, and conditional probability distributions

$$p(y^n), p(\hat{y}^n), p(y^n | \hat{y}^n).$$

The *average distortion* is defined as

$$D = \sum_{y^n} p(y^n) d(y^n, \hat{y}^n).$$

(1.20)

It is possible, using the distributions given above, to define the information transmitted from the incoming Y to the outgoing $\hat{Y}$ process in the usual manner, using the Shannon source uncertainty of the strings:

$$I(Y, \hat{Y}) \equiv H(Y) - H(Y|\hat{Y}) = H(Y) + H(\hat{Y}) - H(Y, \hat{Y}).$$

If there is no uncertainty in Y given the retranslation $\hat{Y}$, then no information is lost.

In general, this will not be true.

The *information rate distortion function* $R(D)$ for a source Y with a distortion measure $d(y, \hat{y})$ is defined as

$$R(D) = \min_{p(y,\hat{y}); \sum_{(y,\hat{y})} p(y)p(y|\hat{y})d(y,\hat{y}) \leq D} I(Y, \hat{Y}).$$

(1.21)

The minimization is over all conditional distributions $p(y|\hat{y})$ for which the joint distribution $p(y, \hat{y}) = p(y)p(y|\hat{y})$ satisfies the average distortion constraint (i.e. average distortion $\leq D$).

The *Rate Distortion Theorem* states that $R(D)$ *is the maximum achievable rate of information transmission which does not exceed the distortion* D. Cover and Thomas (1991) or Dembo and Zeitouni (1998) provide details.

An important observation is that $R(D)$ is necessarily convex in D (Cover and Thomas, 1991, Lemma 13.4.1). This has profound implications for dynamic processes, since R can be interpreted as a free energy homolog, as it is a channel capacity measure.

It is also important to note that pairs of sequences $(y^n, \hat{y}^n)$ can be defined as *distortion typical*; that is, for a given average distortion D, defined in terms of a particular measure, pairs of sequences can be divided into two sets, a high probability one containing a relatively small number of (matched) pairs with $d(y^n, \hat{y}^n) \leq D$, and a low probability one containing most pairs. As $n \to \infty$, the smaller set approaches unit probability, and, for those pairs,

$$p(y^n) \geq p(\hat{y}^n | y^n) \exp[-nI(Y, \hat{Y})].$$

(1.22)

Thus, roughly speaking, $I(Y, \hat{Y})$ embodies the splitting criterion between high and low probability pairs of paths.

For the theory of interacting information sources, then, $I(Y, \hat{Y})$ can play the role of H in a generalized Onsager relations argument.

The rate distortion function can actually be calculated in many cases by using a Lagrange multiplier method – see Section 13.7 of Cover and Thomas (1991).

Glazebrook and Wallace (2009) suggest using something like $s \equiv d(\hat{x}, x)$ as a metric in a geometry of information sources, e.g. when simple ergodicity fails, and $H(x) \neq H(\hat{x})$ for high probability paths $\hat{x}$ and x.

1.8   References

Adami, C., C. Ofria, T. Collier, 2000, Evolution of biological complexity, Proceedings of the National Academy of Sciences, 97:4463-4468.

Adami, C., N. Cerf, 2000, Physical complexity of symbolic sequences, Physica D 137:62-69.

Aldrich, H., G. Hodgson, D. Hull, T. Knudsen, J. Mokyr, and V. Vanberg, 2008, In defense of generalized Darwinism, Journal of Evolutionary Economics 18:577-596.

Atlan, H., Cohen, I., 1998, Immune information, self-organization and meaning, International Immunology 10:711-717.

Ash, R., 1990, Information Theory, Dover, New York.

Beck, C., F. Schlogl, 1993, Thermodynamics of chaotic systems: an introduction, Cambridge University Press, Cambridge, UK.

Champagnat, N., R. Ferriere, S. Meleard, 2006, Unifying evolutionary dynamics: from individual stochastic processes to macroscopic models, Theoretical Population Biology 69:297-321.

Cover T., J. Thomas, 1991, Elements of Information Theory, Wiley, New York.

Dembo, A., O. Zeitouni, 1998, Large Deviations and Applications, Second Edition, Springer, New York.

Diekmann, U., R. Law, 1996, The dynamical theory of coevolution: a derivation from stochastic ecological processes, Journal of Mathematical Biology 34:579-612.

Eldredge, N., S. Gould, 1972, Punctuated equilibrium: an alternative to phyletic gradualism, in T. Schopf (ed.), Models in Paleobiology, Freeman, Cooper and Co., San Francisco, pp. 82-115.

Feynman, R., 2000, Lectures on Computation, Westview Press, New York.

Fodor, J., M. Piatelli-Palmarini, 2010, What Darwin got wrong, Farrar, Straus, and Giroux, New York.

Glazebrook, J.F., R. Wallace, 2009, Rate distortion manifolds as models for cognitive information, Informatica 33:309-345.

Gould, S., 2002, The Structure of Evolutionary Theory, Harvard University Press, Cambridge, MA.

Haldane, A., R. May, 2011, Systemic risk in banking ecosystems, Nature 469:351-355.

Hodgson, G., T. Knudsen, 2010, Darwin's Conjecture: The search for general principles of social and economic evolution, University of Chicago Press.

Holling, C., 1992, Cross-scale morphology, geometry and dynamics of ecosystems, Ecological Monographs 62:447-502.

Johnson, N., 2011, Proposing policy by analogy is risky, Nature 469:302-303.

Khinchin, A., 1957, Mathematical Foundations of Information Theory, Dover, New York.

Levin, 1989, Ecology in theory and application, in S. Levin, T. Hallam, L. Gross (eds.), Applied Mathematical Ecology, Biomathematics texts Vol. 18, Springer, New York.

Lewontin, R., 2010, Not so natural selection, New York Review of Books online.

Odling-Smee, F., K. Laland, M. Feldman, 2003, Niche Construction: The neglected process in evolution. Princeton University Press, Princeton, N.J.

Ofria, C. Adami, T. Collier, 2003, Selective pressures on genomes in molecular evolution, Journal of Theoretical Biology 222:62-69.

Pielou, E., 1977, Mathematical Ecology, John Wiley and Sons, New York.

Wallace, R., R. G. Wallace, 2008, On the spectrum of prebiotic chemical systems: an information-theoretic treatment of Eigen's Paradox, Origins of Life and Evolution of Biospheres 38:419-455.

Wallace, R., D. Wallace, 2008, Punctuated equilibrium in statistical models of generalized coevolutionary resilience, Transactions on Computational Systems Biology IX LNBI 5121 23-85.

Wallace, R., D. Wallace, 2009, Code, context and epigenetic catalysis in gene expression, Transactions on Computational Systems Biology XI, LNBI 5750 283-334.

Wallace, R., D. Wallace, R.G. Wallace, 2009, Farming Human Pathogens: Ecological Resilience and Evolutionary Process, Springer, New York.

Wallace, R., D. Wallace, 2010, Gene Expression and its Discontents: The Social Production of Chronic Disease, Springer, New York.

Wallace, R., 2005, Consciousness: A Mathematical Treatment of the Global Neuronal Workspace Model, Springer, New York.

Wallace, R., 2010, Expanding the modern synthesis, Comptes Rendus Biologies 333:701-709.

Wymer, C., 1997, Structural nonlinear continuous-time models in econometrics, Macroeconomic Dynamics 1:518-548.

Zhu, R., A. Rebirio, D. Salahub, S. Kaufmann, 2007, Studying genetic regulatory networks at the molecular level: delayed reaction stochastic models, Journal of Theoretical Biology 246:725-745.

Chapter 2

Niche construction

2.1 Introduction

Expanding the Modern Evolutionary Synthesis requires elevating the role of interaction within and across various biological scales to the status of an evolutionary principle. One way to do this is to characterize genes, gene expression, and embedding environment as information sources linked by crosstalk, constrained by the asymptotic limit theorems of information theory (Wallace, 2010a). This produces an inherently interactive structure that escapes the constraints of mathematical population genetics and other replicator dynamics. The first chapter makes application of this perspective to economic process, viewing the heritage system of the firm, the cognitive process by which the firm responds to patterns of threat and opportunity in a way that must be consistent with that heritage, and the embedding economic environment, as interacting information sources. Here we examine the fitness of the firm from that larger perspective, finding it to be intimately intertwined with niche construction – the process by which the firm adapts the immediate environment to its needs. Two complementary models are explored: niche construction as mediating the connection between environmental signals and the cognitive functioning of the firm, and as a means of tuning the channel for the transmission of heritage and other information in a noisy environment. These are different views of the same elephant, in a sense, seen as simplified projections down from the larger dynamic system of the previous chapter.

That is, we restrict the theory to recover a closer analog to conventional selection and fitness theory, inherently modified, however, by processes of niche construction (e.g., Odling-Smee et al., 2003) analogous to biofilms, multicellularity, burrows, eusocial nests, and larger social formations that mediate between individual development and environmental signals. This perspective recovers something much like the fitness concept of traditional evolutionary theory.

Processes of niche construction, in economic terms, might include the establishment of, and active participation in, trade associations and 'standards' bodies, whose lobbying and regulatory activities smooth the path for firms in a particular industry. Advertising is clearly another such mode. Similar activities could involve special discounts to favored clients, the use of social networks for marketing, the payment of bribes, the suborning of trade unions, the enlistment of de-facto goon squads against competitors or reluctant clients, and so on. Empirical indices of these latter activities might include legal fees and records of prosecution.

2.2 Niche construction 1

2.2.1 Preliminaries

The basic schema is that of figure 2.1. A multifactorial environmental signal, a 'message', $y^n = \{y_1, y_1, ..., y_n\}$, representing the systematic output of the embedding economic ecosystem information source, is expressed by an information source representing the cognitive response of the firm to that embedding ecosystem in terms of a multifactorial pattern of behavioral phenotypes chosen from some set $\{S_1, ..., S_m\}$ that becomes the serial 'message' $b^n = \{b_1, b_2, ..., b_n\}$. We deterministically retranslate, 'decode', the phenotype message b^n to produce a new version of the original environmental message, i.e., the environment inferred from the firm's phenotype expressions. Write that inferred picture as $\hat{y}^n = \{\hat{y}_1, \hat{y}_2, ..., \hat{y}_n\}$. Next, introduce a numerical distortion measure that compares y_i with $\hat{y}_i$, writing it as $d(y_i, \hat{y}_i)$. As Cover and Thomas (1991) indicate, as summarized in the Mathematical Appendix of the previous chapter, many such measures are possible and have been used, and the essential dynamics are, remarkably, independent of the precise measure chosen.

Suppose that with each path y^n and b^n-path retranslation into the y language, $\hat{y}^n$, there are associated individual, joint, and conditional probability distributions $p(y^n), p(\hat{y}^n), p(y^n, \hat{y}^n), p(y^n|\hat{p}^n)$.

The average distortion is defined as

$$D = \sum_{y^n} p(y^n) d(y^n, \hat{y}^n).$$

(2.1)

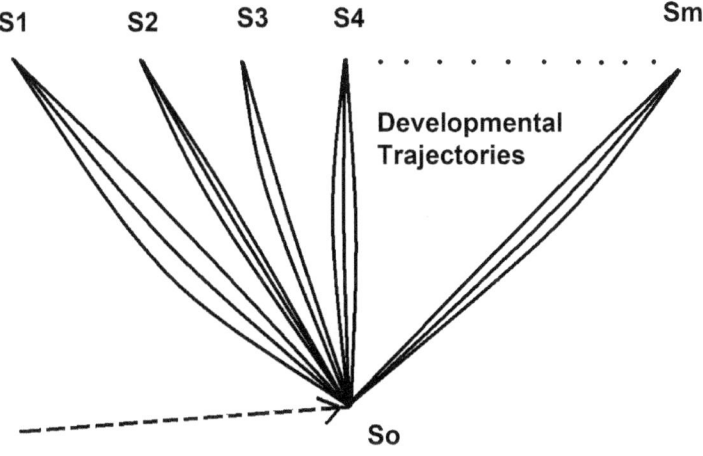

Multifactorial phenotype expression of environmental message {b1, b2, ..., bn}

Spectrum of possible phenotypes

S1 S2 S3 S4 Sm

Developmental Trajectories

So

Multifactorial environmental mesage {y1, y2, ..., yn}

Figure 2.1: An environmental 'message' $y = \{y_1, y_2, ..., y_n\}$ is expressed as a response 'message' $b = \{b_1, b_2, ..., b_n\}$ in terms of the possible 'phenotypes' from the underlying set $\{S_1, ..., S_m\}$, that is deterministically translated into a reconstruction of the environmental message written as $\hat{y}$. A distortion measure $d(y, \hat{y})$ characterizes the difference between what was sent and what was received, allowing construction of an average distortion D, inversely measuring fitness, and a rate distortion function $R(D)$ that permits analysis in terms of an index of available free energy.

Clearly, D *is an inverse fitness measure*: phenotypes that match environments produce higher rates of successful persistence of the firm, in this model.

It is possible, using the distributions above, to define the information transmitted from the Y to the $\hat{Y}$ process using the Shannon source uncertainty of the strings:

$$I(Y,\hat{Y}) = H(Y) - H(Y|\hat{Y}) = H(Y) + H(\hat{Y}) - H(Y,\hat{Y}),$$

(2.2)

where $H(...,...)$ is the standard joint, and $H(...|...)$ the conditional, Shannon uncertainties (Cover and Thomas, 1991, Ash, 1990). If there is no uncertainty in Y given the retranslation $\hat{Y}$, then no information has been lost, and the systems are in perfect synchrony. In general, of course, this will not be true, and information has been lost in the translation of the environmental message into final phenotype spectrum.

The *rate distortion function* $R(D)$ for a source Y with a distortion measure $d(y,\hat{y})$ is defined as

$$R(D) = \min_{p(y,\hat{y}); \sum_{(y,\hat{y})} p(y)p(y|\hat{y})d(y,\hat{y}) \leq D} I(Y,\hat{Y}).$$

(2.3)

The minimization is over all conditional distributions $p(y|\hat{y})$ for which the joint distribution $p(y,\hat{y}) = p(y)p(y|\hat{y})$ satisfies the average distortion constraint (i.e., average distortion $\leq D$).

The *Rate Distortion Theorem* states that $R(D)$ is the minimum necessary rate of information transmission that ensures the communication between systems of interest does not exceed average distortion D. Thus $R(D)$ defines a minimum necessary channel capacity. Cover and Thomas (1991) or Dembo and Zeitouni (1998) provide details.

The rate distortion function has been calculated for a number of systems.

An absolutely central fact characterizes the rate distortion function: Cover and Thomas (1991, Lemma 13.4.1) show that $R(D)$ *is necessarily a decreasing convex function of D for any reasonable definition of distortion.*

That is, $R(D)$ *is always* a reverse J-shaped curve. This will prove crucial for the overall argument. Indeed, convexity is an exceedingly powerful mathematical condition, and permits deep inference (e.g., Rockafellar, 1970). Ellis (1985, Ch. VI) applies convexity theory to conventional statistical mechanics.

For a Gaussian channel having noise with zero mean and variance σ^2 (Cover and Thomas, 1991),

$$R(D) = 1/2 \log[\sigma^2/D], 0 < D \leq \sigma^2$$

$$R(D) = 0, D > \sigma^2.$$

(2.4)

For a Poisson channel with message arrival rate λ – essentially information transmission by an analog to photon counting in which the instantaneous output rate is controlled by the input modulo noise – the rate distortion function is (Bedekar, 2001)

$$R(D) = \log[1/\lambda D], 0 < D \leq 1/\lambda$$

$$R(D) = 0, D > 1/\lambda$$

(2.5)

where D is the average in-order service time of a hypothetical first come first serve queue that would result in the output.

Recall, now, the relation between information source uncertainty and channel capacity (e.g., Ash, 1990),$H[X] \leq C$, where H is the uncertainty of the source X and C the channel capacity, defined according to the relation (Ash, 1990)

$$C \equiv \max_{P(X)} I(X|Y),$$

(2.6)

where $P(X)$ is chosen so as to maximize the rate of information transmission along a channel Y.

Also recall the analogous definition of the rate distortion function above, again an extremum over a probability distribution.

Likewise, recall the homology between information source uncertainty and free energy density. If $N(n)$ is the number of high probability 'meaningful' – that is, grammatical and syntactical – sequences of length n emitted by an information source X, then, according to the Shannon-McMillan Theorem, the zero-error limit of the Rate Distortion Theorem (Ash, 1990; Cover and Thomas, 1991; Khinchin, 1957),

$$H[X] = \lim_{n \to \infty} \frac{\log[N(n)]}{n}$$

$$= \lim_{n \to \infty} H(X_n | X_0, ..., X_{n-1})$$

$$= \lim_{n \to \infty} \frac{H(X_0, ..., X_n)}{n+1},$$

(2.7)

where, again, $H(...|...)$ is the conditional and $H(..., ...)$ is the joint Shannon uncertainty.

Finally, recall the 'free energy' argument of the first chapter: In the limit of large n, $H[X]$ becomes homologous to the free energy density of a physical system at the thermodynamic limit of infinite volume. More explicitly, the free energy density of a physical system having volume V and partition function $Z(\beta)$ derived from the system's Hamiltonian

– the energy function – at inverse temperature β is (e.g., Landau and Lifshitz 2007)

$$F[K] = \lim_{V \to \infty} -\frac{1}{\beta} \frac{\log[Z(\beta, V)]}{V} \equiv$$

$$\lim_{V \to \infty} \frac{\log[\hat{Z}(\beta, V)]}{V},$$

(2.8)

with $\hat{Z} = Z^{-1/\beta}$. The latter expression is formally similar to the first part of equation (2.7), a circumstance having deep implications: Feynman (2000) describes in great detail how information and free energy have an inherent duality. Feynman, in fact, defines information precisely as the free energy needed to erase a message. The argument is surprisingly direct (e.g., Bennett, 1988), and for very simple systems it is easy to design a small (idealized) machine that turns the information within a message directly into usable work – free energy. Information is a form of free energy and the construction and transmission of information within living things consumes metabolic free energy, with nearly inevitable losses via the second law of thermodynamics. If there are limits on available metabolic free energy there will necessarily be limits on the ability to process information, and in particular to match phenotype expression to environmental cues.

2.2.2 A first model

$R(D)$ is, by this account, a dimensionless free energy measure, constrained by the availability of metabolic free energy, in a large sense. We therefore, as a first approximation, write a probability density function for the average distortion D – an inverse fitness measure – as driven by the classic Gibbs relation

$$\exp[-R/Q(\kappa M)],$$

where M is a measure of available free energy, κ an inverse energy scaling constant, and $Q(\kappa M)$ is monotonic increasing with $Q(0) = 0$.
    Then

$$P[D] = \frac{\exp[-R(D)/Q(\kappa M)]dR(D)/dD}{\int_0^{max} \exp[-R(D)/Q(\kappa M)]dR(D)/dDdD}$$

(2.9)

Higher M, in this model, permits lower average distortion, and we can find the mean of the average distortion – again, an inverse index of fitness – as a function of M.

For the Gaussian channel, direct calculation gives

$$< D_G >= \int DP[D]dD = \frac{\sigma^2}{2Q(\kappa M)+1}.$$

(2.10)

Note here that, if, for example, $Q(\kappa M) = \sqrt[n]{\kappa M}$, then

$$\kappa M = [\frac{1}{2}(\frac{\sigma^2}{<D>} - 1)]^n,$$

and high fitness – small $< D >$ – can require enormous rates of metabolic free energy, if σ^2 is not very small.

For the Poisson channel,

$$< D_P >= \frac{1/\lambda}{Q(\kappa M)+1}.$$

(2.11)

According to this model, $< D >$, representing an inverse fitness measure, that is, how well a dynamical structure can represent environmental signals, depends on both critical internal parameters such as σ^2 and λ, and on the exact form of $Q(\kappa M)$.

This result has significant implications for understanding niche construction: in the sense of a recent treatment of intrinsically disordered proteins in a rough folding funnel (Wallace, 2010b), niche construction 'self-lubricates' or impedance-matches the relation between cognitive corporate functioning and environmental demands, decreasing σ^2 or increasing λ, according the nature of the channel, thus reducing the expenditure of analogs to metabolic free energy that are needed to lower D, and hence to increase fitness.

The analysis has been based on the Gibbs relation, defining probabilities in terms of $\exp[-R(D)/Q(\kappa M)]$, where R is the rate distortion function and Q an index of available 'metabolic free energy', in a large sense. A more general model emerges from viewing $R(D)$ itself as a free energy measure, generating an empirical Onsager equation something like equation (1.4).

Define an entropy analog from $R(D)$ as

$$S_R \equiv R(D) - D dR(D)/dD.$$

(2.12)

The simplest Onsager relation is then

$$dD/dt = -\mu dS_R/dD.$$

(2.13)

For the Gaussian channel, with $R(D) = 1/2 \log[\sigma^2/D]$,

$$dD/dt = -\mu dS_R/dD = \mu/2D,$$

having the solution

$$D(t) = \sqrt{\mu t}.$$

(2.14)

This is the classic diffusion result of Einstein: In the absence of input that may range from information to consumables and other 'free energy' resources, the firm departs from the demands of the embedding environment at a rate proportional to the square root of the time. For the Poisson channel, $D(t) = \sqrt{2\mu t}$.

In the presence of 'free energy' resources, the Onsager equation becomes

$$dD/dt = -\mu dS_R/dD - F(\kappa M),$$

(2.15)

so that, for the Gaussian channel at equilibrium, when $dD/dt = 0$,

$$0 = \mu/2D_{equilib} - F(\kappa M)$$

$$D_{equilib} = \frac{\mu}{2F(\kappa M)}.$$

(2.16)

Choosing $F \equiv \mu(2Q(\kappa M) + 1)/2\sigma^2$ gives equation (2.10),

$$D_{equilib} = \frac{\sigma^2}{2Q(\kappa M) + 1}.$$

(2.17)

Using the general method, however, outcomes beyond the Gibbs relation are possible.

2.3   Spontaneous symmetry breaking

Taking $R(D)$ as a free energy measure constrained by the availability of metabolic free energy that is itself a temperature analog, we have shown that one can invoke something much like empirical Onsager equations that are not restricted to the Gibbs format based on $\exp[-R/Q]$. More results in this direction are possible.

Suppose that, in response to environmental clues, adaptive phenotypes – behaviors of the firm – can occur in recognizable equivalence classes. For example, tracking, say, a decline in average demand, a coordinated set of responses emerges: cutbacks, searches for greater efficiency, cheaper sources of raw materials, and so on. Equivalence classes, by standard arguments (e.g., Brown, 1987; Weinstein, 1996), generate groupoids, and groupoids permit adoption of Pettini's (2007) topological hypothesis, a variant of Landau's perspective on phase transition. Recall, first, that the simplest groupoid is just a disjoint union of groups, and the generalization to equivalence classes is direct. Second, under these circumstances, R can itself be taken as a Morse Function (e.g., Pettini, 2007; Matsumoto, 2002). Thus Pettini's arguments are directly applicable, so that fundamental topological changes in phenotype structure are a necessary, but not sufficient, index of phase transition. The outline is as follows.

The essence of Landau's insight on phase transitions (e.g., Landau and Lifshitz, 2007) is that certain of them take place in the context of symmetry change, with one phase, at higher temperature, being more symmetric than the other. A symmetry is lost in the transition. The highest possible set of symmetries is that of the Hamiltonian describing the energy states. States accessible at lower temperatures will not have the symmetries available at higher temperatures, and the transitions will be highly punctuated. Pettini (2007) expands this argument in a formal Morse-theoretic framework.

Taking R itself as the 'free energy' Morse Function, and $Q(\kappa M)$ as the 'temperature'-analog, in the context of a groupoid structure for equivalence classes of phenotype responses, gives the result.

Further exploration of this kind of argument is given in the next chapter.

2.4   Niche construction 2

A quite different picture of niche construction emerges from application of the 'tuning' version of Shannon's Coding Theorem, as described in the Mathematical Appendix to Chapter 1, to instantiate a Rate Distortion Manifold (Glazebrook and Wallace, 2009a, b). The basic argument follows that of Wallace et al., (2009, Section 2.10).

The focus is now on the successful transmission of information within a noisy environmental channel, and the role of niche construction in tuning that channel. For a Gaussian channel characterized by a simple environmental parameter, the added noise σ^2, this becomes another form of impedance-matching lubrication, in the sense of the previous sections.

Messages from an information source, seen as symbols x_j from some alphabet, each having probabilities P_j associated with a random variable X, are encoded into the language of some transmission channel, a random variable Y with symbols y_k, having probabilities P_k, possibly with error. The received symbol y_k is then retranslated – decoded – (without error) into some x_k, which may or may not be the same as the x_j that was sent.

Recall that the capacity of the channel is defined according to equation (2.6), i.e., $C \equiv \max_{P(X)} I(X|Y)$, subject to the subsidiary condition that $\sum P(X) = 1$.

Recall also that the critical trick of the Shannon Coding Theorem for sending a message with arbitrarily small error along the channel Y at any rate $R < C$ is to encode it in longer and longer 'typical' sequences of the variable X; that is, those sequences whose distribution of symbols approximates the probability distribution $P(X)$ above which maximizes C.

If $S(n)$ is the number of such 'typical' sequences of length n, then $\log[S(n)] \approx nH(X)$, where $H(X)$ is the uncertainty of the stochastic variable defined above. Some consideration shows that $S(n)$ is much less than the total number of possible messages of length n. Thus, as $n \to \infty$, only a vanishingly small fraction of all possible messages is meaningful in this sense. This observation, after some considerable development, is what allows the Coding Theorem to work so well. In sum, the prescription is to encode messages in typical sequences, that are sent at very nearly the capacity of the channel. As the encoded messages become longer and longer, their maximum possible rate of transmission without error approaches channel capacity as a limit. Again, Ash (1990), Khinchin (1957) and Cover and Thomas (1991) provide details.

This approach can be, in a sense, inverted to give a tuning theorem that parsimoniously describes the essence of the Rate Distortion Manifold. As the Mathematical Appendix to Chapter 1 demonstrates, in a purely formal mathematical sense, the message transmits the channel, and there will indeed be, according to the Shannon Coding Theorem, a channel distribution $P(Y)$ which maximizes C^*.

One may, as described previously, do better than this, however, by modifying the channel matrix $P(Y|X)$, in our case, via niche construction. Since $P(y_j) = \sum_{i=1}^{M} P(x_i)P(y_j|x_i)$, $P(Y)$ is entirely defined by the channel matrix $P(Y|X)$ for fixed $P(X)$ and

$$C^* = \max_{P(Y),P(Y|X)} I(Y|X) = \max_{P(Y|X)} I(Y|X).$$

(2.18)

The essential point is that, *for the transmission of information in a noisy environment, niche construction provides a means to tune the transmitting channel around the message.*

Some further insight to this process can be found by examining a Gaussian channel, now focusing on the channel capacity rather than on the distortion, as in the previous sections. Channel capacity is, here, a direct measure of fitness. The analysis for a Poisson channel is similar, but more algebraically involved.

We assume a real number coarse graining for the index of interest, represented by a stochastic variate X, acting under a 'power constraint' such that the expectation of X^2 is limited: $E(X^2) \leq \mathcal{P} > 0$. If σ^2 is the variance in the (zero-mean) noise affecting the channel, then the channel capacity, the maximum rate at which information can be transmitted, is given by the relation (Cover and Thomas, 1991)

$$C = \frac{1}{2} \log[1 + \frac{\mathcal{P}}{\sigma^2}].$$

(2.19)

Here, again, C is a direct fitness measure, in contrast to the average distortion D of the previous section, and we would expect $\mathcal{P} = Q(\kappa M)$ as above, so that

$$C = \frac{1}{2} \log[1 + \frac{Q(\kappa M)}{\sigma^2}].$$

(2.20)

Tuning the channel – impedance matching lubrication by niche construction, in this model – is equivalent to *decreasing* the noise σ^2, increasing the effectiveness of a given level of available metabolic energy, M.

Indeed, the arguments of section 2.2 might well be reformulated form this perspective.

2.5   Available free energy

Equations (2.10), (2.11), and (2.20) relate a monotonic increasing function of available metabolic free energy to the ability of a firm to adapt to environmental signals and to faithfully transmit internal heritage information in a noisy environment. Consideration suggests that such a concept involves three interacting phenomena, (1) the quality of information received from the embedding environment (external or internal), (2) the quality of resources accessible to respond to the signals sent by the embedding environment(s), and (3) the efficiency with which information or resources can be applied within the culture of the firm. This implies a synergistic relation of the form

$M \propto$ Corporate Efficiency $\times$ Information Quality $\times$ Resource Availability.

All three factors are profoundly affected by the cognitive functioning of the firm that may, as described in Wallace and Fullilove (2008), depend on the ability of multiple global workspace broadcasts within the firm to engage with each other. This represents a kind of slow-speed multiple personality collective consciousness that requires considerable mathematical overhead for adequate description. The essential points revolve around the ability of the multiple workspace broadcasts to both interact efficiently and have enough diversity to avoid the trap of inattentional blindness (e.g., Wallace, 2007). Details of the pathologies of cognitive process within the firm can be found in Wallace and Fullilove (2008). A summary of the basic ideas is as follows:

The central ideas of Global Workspace theory (Baars and Franklin, 2003) are that

(1) The brain can be viewed as a collection of distributed specialized networks (processors).

(2) Consciousness is associated with a global workspace in the brain – a fleeting memory capacity whose focal contents are widely distributed (broadcast) to many unconscious specialized networks.

(3) Conversely, a global workspace can also serve to integrate many competing and cooperating input networks.

(4) Some unconscious networks, called contexts, shape conscious contents. For example, unconscious parietal maps modulate visual feature cells that underlie the perception of color in the ventral stream.

(5) Such contexts work together jointly to constrain conscious events.

(6) Motives and emotions can be viewed as goal contexts.

(7) Executive functions work as hierarchies of goal contexts.

Agent-based and artificial neural network (ANN) treatments of cognition, consciousness and other higher order mental functions, taking Krebs' (2005) view, are *sufficiency* arguments, mimicking mentality without providing real understanding of the underlying structure in the same way that a Fourier series can approximate a function over a fixed interval. The Ptolemaic theory of the solar system, an Earth-centered paradigm, required epicycle upon epicycle to approximate the dynamic behaviors of the planets. A sun-centered Keplerian system provides instant simplicity and deep understanding.

Necessary conditions, as Dretske (1994) argues, give considerably more insight. They are conditions to which all cognitive phenomena must assimilate, and they are in no small part characterized by the asymptotic limit theorems of information theory.

Wallace and Fullilove (2008) study Baars' theme from Dretske's viewpoint, finding the necessary conditions which the asymptotic limit theorems of information theory impose on the global workspace. These, it can be shown, impose constraints on individual consciousness – what Baars calls *contexts*. Information theory methods, extended by a homology between information source uncertainty and the free energy density of a physical system, formally account for the effects on individual consciousness of parallel physiological modules such as the immune system, embedding structures such as the local social network, and, most importantly, the cultural heritages that mark human biology. Neuron firing alone, although certainly a part of the whole, does not comprise the totality of mental function. Consciousness, a higher-order function, is the provenance of an entire animal, including, for many species, its social context.

Understanding the linking of unconscious cognitive submodules can be done through a transfer phase change approaches from statistical physics to information theory via the same homology between information source uncertainty and free energy density. The transfer cleanly generates a punctuated accession to consciousness. The renormalization calculation focuses on a phase transition that arises from a change in the average strength of nondisjunctive weak ties (*sensu* Granovetter, 1973) linking the unconscious submodules. A second-order universality class tuning allows for adaptation of conscious attention via rate distortion manifolds. A version of the Baars model (including contexts) emerges as an almost exact parallel to hierarchical regression, based, however, on the Shannon-McMillan Theorem rather than the Central Limit Theorem on which most modern-day modeling depends.

Wallace and Fullilove (2008) use classic results from random and semirandom network theory (e.g., Albert and Barabasi, 2002) applied to a modular network of cognitive processors. The method provides a foundation for a different, but roughly parallel, treatment of the global workspace to that given in Wallace (2005). In fact there can be intermediate models, as well as those acting at very slow rates. This suggests an equivalence class structure for global workspace models, and the possibility of a number of different mechanisms that can achieve such large-scale structure and dynamics.

Wallace and Fullilove (2008) show it is possible to use renormalization parameters to tune the threshold at which a giant component, or set of them, emerges, along with its topological structure, by way of an iteration involving a tunable rate distortion manifold retina-analog. The treatment generalizes Newell's (1990) blackboard model to give a highly flexible, indeed tunable, version of Baars' broadcast mechanism across many possible underlying neural topologies. Wallace (2005), by contrast, uses 'universality class tuning' to direct the phase transitions associated with changing the average strength of weak ties between modules.

These approaches together offer different analytically tractable asymptotic limits in a much larger domain of possible models.

Although both kinds of linkage are sufficient to produce large-scale connectivity or general broadcast, another iteration seems required to produce higher cognitive function. Some second level models may be more amenable to such iteration than others.

Again, there are two quite distinct analytically treatable models of this general broadcast mechanism that both instantiate Baars' global workspace model, the *mean field* model of nondisjunctive linkage between linked cognitive modules, and the *mean number* model of such linkages.

The two contrasting treatments both produce very similar tunable broadcasts comparable to the Baars global workspace model of consciousness. Less mathematically tractable intermediate structures seem possible, in which both average strength and average numbers of crosstalk linkages can vary and tune the broadcast. Evolution, be it biological or social, however, does not seem particularly constrained by mathematical tractability.

A groupoid approach permits development of a system that entertains several, even many, simultaneous workspaces able to initiate global broadcasts. An obvious canonical failure mode of such a structure involves miscommunication between workspaces: The Rate Distortion Theorem states that there is an inherent limit on the transmission rate for any specified level of average distortion. Too rapid 'handoff' at shift change, for example, guarantees great distortion.

A second canonical failure mode for such systems is inattentional blindness, i.e., overfocus by the generalized retina of a tunable rate distortion manifold, which might be lessened by the existence of multiple, different, simultaneous workspaces, but would remain acute under policies of enforced institutional or organizational conformity which would eliminate multiple perspectives on incoming 'sensory' data.

A third involves a pathological 'lock-in' to non-adaptive dynamic topological modes similar to the eutrophication of a natural ecosystem: ecological as opposed to engineering resilience. Engineering resilience supposes graceful degradation under stress, followed by return to normal. Ecosystem resilience sees stress causing sudden, relatively permanent, shifts to possibly pathological modes.

Such shifts may, indeed, be driven by 'Red Queen' effects analogous to competitive failure dynamics in a market economy, particularly inverse 'Pentagon Ratchet' mechanisms driven by feedback between institutional distributed cognition and a closely coupled embedding cultural milieu.

2.6 Fitness of the firm

Taking a corporate cognition/environment perspective, according to equations (2.10) and (2.11), a firm whose ability to respond to environmental signals, to match corporate behavioral or structural phenotypes to the demands of an embedding economic ecosystem, is constrained by channel capacity – high noise σ^2 or low signal rate λ – must inevitably suffer diminished fitness, requiring considerable 'metabolic free energy' to adapt the corporate developmental trajectory to selection pressures.

But what of a firm that can interact, in a hierarchical manner, with the embedding economic environment, in the sense of principle (5)? In a purely biological context, biofilms, multicellularity, burrows, eusocial nests, herds, and the more structured social assemblages of the hominids and their cultures, all provide means to limit noise or increase signal strength, by, essentially, impedance matching environment to development. That is, examining the fitness of the firm in terms of its constructed niche decreases an 'effective' σ^2 and increases an 'effective' λ in equations (2.10) and (2.11), representing increased fitness in terms of decreased distortion in the channel between the firm and an embedding environment now primarily represented by the constructed niche.

Another way of looking at this is to say that it is the hierarchical structure of firm-in-niche that interacts with the environment, now via impedance-matching effective parameters.

Looking at the transmission of information in a noisy environment – a quite different view – Section 2.4 suggests that niche construction can also be viewed as a means of tuning the heritage information transmission channel so as to maximize the fidelity of the heritage message. For a simple Gaussian channel, equation (2.20) shows such tuning can sometimes be viewed as another form of impedance-matching lubrication.

These are, then, complementary perspectives that describe the same process via added epicycles to the limited machinery of the first four principles of the Modern Evolutionary Synthesis, as described in the first chapter. Introduction of principle (5), incorporating environmental interaction, collapses the argument, in the sense of the previous chapter, and subsumes both models, providing a more complete picture of the entire elephant, in a manner of speaking, at the expense of the considerable mathematical machinery inherent to equation (1.4).

Introducing higher order embedding culture directly into the model of the previous chapter is most simply done by invoking a fourth information source – the larger culture as a generalized language – into equation (1.4). The argument is direct, although the effects are likely to be most subtle.

Clearly, then, the introduction of principle (5) permits introduction into formal theory of at least some of the immense amount of social and economic process that is missing from current formal versions of economics. Most critically, ideas of fitness and niche construction must become intimately intertwined in any such expanded formulation.

2.7 References

Albert, R., A. Barabasi, 2002, Statistical mechanics of complex networks, Reviews of Modern Physics, 74:47-97.

Ash, R., 1990, Information Theory, Dover, New York.

Avital, E., E. Jablonka, 2000, Animal Traditions: Behavioral Inheritance in Evolution, Cambridge University Press, NY.

Baars, B., Franklin, S., 2003, How conscious experience and working memory interact. Trends in Cognitive Science, 7:166-172.

Bedekar, A., 2001, On the information about message arrival times required for in-order decoding. In Proceedings of the International Symposium on Information Theory (ISIT), Washington, DC, 2201:227.

Bennett, C., 1988, Logical depth and physical complexity. In R. Herkin (ed.), The Universal Turing Machine: A Half-Century Survey, Oxford University Press, pp. 227-257.

Brown, R., 1987, From groups to groupoids: a brief survey. Bulletin of the London Mathematical Society, 19:113-134.

Champagnat, N., R. Ferriere, S. Meleard, 2006, Unifying evolutionary dynamics: From individual stochastic processes to macroscopic models, Theoretical Population Biology, 69:297-321.

Cover, T., J. Thomas, 1991, Elements of Information Theory, Wiley, New York.

Dembo, A., O. Zeitouni, 1998, Large Deviations and Applications, 2nd. edn., Springer, NY.

Dretske, F., 1994, The explanatory role of information, Philosophical Transactions of the Royal Society A, 349:59-70.

Eldredge, N., S. Gould, 1972, Punctuated equilibrium: an alternative to phyletic gradualism. In T. Schopf (ed.), Models in Paleobiology, 82-115, Freeman, Cooper and Co., San Francisco.

Ellis, R., 1985, Entropy, Large Deviations, and Statistical Mechanics, Springer, New York.

Feynman, R., 2000, Lectures on Computation, Westview, New York.

Glazebrook, J.F., R. Wallace, 2009a, Small worlds and Red Queens in the global workspace: an information theoretic approach, Cognitive Systems Research, 10:333-365.

Glazebrook, J.F., R. Wallace, 2009b Rate distortion manifolds as models for cognitive information, Informatica, 33:309-345.

Granovetter, M., 1973, The strength of weak ties, American Journal of Sociology, 78:1360-1380.

Khinchin, A., 1957, Mathematical Foundations of Information Theory, Dover, New York.

Krebs, P., 2005, Models of cognition: neurological possibility does not indicate neurological plausibility. In Bara, B., L. Barsalou, M. Buddiarelli (eds.), Proceedings of CogSci 2005, pp. 1184-1189, Stresa, Italy. Available at http://cogprints.org/4498/.

Landau, L., E. Lifshitz, 2007, Statistical Physics, Part I, Elsevier, New York.

Lewontin, R., 2010, Not so natural selection, New York Review of Books Online, May 27.

Matsumoto, Y., 2002, An Introduction to Morse Theory. Translations of Mathematical Monographs, Vol. 208, The American Mathematical Society.

Newell, A., 1990, Unified Theories of Cognition, Harvard University Press, Cambridge, MA.

Odling-Smee, F., K. Laland, M. Feldman, 2003, Niche Construction: The Neglected Process in Evolution, Princeton University Press, N.J.

Pettini, M., 200), Geometry and Topology in Hamiltonian Dynamics and Statistical Mechanics, Springer, New York.

Rockefellar, R., 1970, Convex Analysis, Princeton University Press, Princeton, NJ.

Wallace, R., M. Fullilove, 2008, Collective Consciousness and its Discontents: Institutional Distributed Cognition, Racial Policy and Public Health in the United States, Springer, New York.

Wallace, R., D. Wallace, 2008, Punctuated equilibrium in statistical models of generalized coevolutionary resilience: how sudden ecosystem transitions can entrain both phenotype expression and Darwinian selection, Transactions on Computational Systems Biology IX, LNBI 5121: 23-85.

Wallace, R., D. Wallace, 2009, Code, context, and epigenetic catalysis in gene expression, Transactions on Computational Systems Biology XI, LNBI 5750: 283-334.

Wallace, R., D. Wallace, 2010, Gene Expression and Its Discontents: The Social Production of Chronic Disease, Springer, New York.

Wallace, R., D. Wallace, R.G. Wallace, 2010, Farming Human Pathogens: Ecological Resilience and Evolutionary Process, Springer, New York.

Wallace, R., 2005, Consciousness: a mathematical treatment of the global neuronal workspace model, Springer, New York.

Wallace, R., 2007, Culture and inattentional blindness: a global workspace perspective, Journal of Theoretical Biology, 245:378-390.

Wallace, R., 2010a, Expanding the modern synthesis, Comptes Rendus Biologies, 333:701-709.

Wallace, R., 2010b, Structure and dynamics of the 'protein folding code' inferred using Tlusty's topological rate distortion approach, BioSystems, 103:18-26..

Weinstein, A., 1996, Groupoids: unifying internal and external symmetry, Notices of the American Mathematical Association, 43:744-752.

Chapter 3

Farming an economy

3.1 Introduction

Haldane and May (2011), taking the 'econophysics' perspective of Caccioli et al. (2009), recently explored risk in banking ecosystems, adopting tools from network theory to study the effects of interaction between individual subcomponents leading to the propagation of shocks within large-scale financial structures. Other approaches to the origin and propagation of such 'shocks' arise more naturally from the generalized Darwinian perspectives of Aldrich et al. (2008) and Hodgson and Knudsen (2010), based on a necessary-conditions application of the Modern Evolutionary Synthesis to economic phenomena.

Wallace (2010a) has proposed expanding the Modern Synthesis itself by introducing 'The principle of environmental interaction,' i.e., that individuals and groups engage in powerful, often punctuated, dynamic mutual relations with their embedding environments that may include the exchange of heritage material between markedly different organisms. Others have taken a similar perspective, without using the constraints available from information theory (e.g., Gabora and Aerts, 2005, 2007). The previous chapters apply the expanded model to the generalized Darwinism of Hodgson and Knudsen (2010). The approach characterizes the heritage system of the firm, the cognitive process by which the firm responds to patterns of threat and opportunity, and embedding socioeconomic environment, as interacting information sources constrained by the asymptotic limit theorems of information theory. This leads to an inherently coevolutionary system described in terms of a formalism quite similar to that of Onsager's nonequilibrium thermodynamics, having quasi-stable 'coevolutionary' states coupled by highly structured large deviations, all much in the sense of Champagnat et al. (2006). The possibility arises that such structured large deviations, rather than merely expressing the self-dynamic processes of a language that speaks itself, can be harnessed by an external 'farmer', that is, regulated to produce a directed socioeconomic ecosystem akin to the primitive neolithic agriculture that enabled the construction of richer social and cultural milieus.

The previous chapters introduce powerful methods from the statistical physics of phase transitions into generalized Darwinian evolutionary theory, much in the spirit of the recent paper by Goldenfeld and Woese (2010), who focus on evolution 'as a problem in nonequilibrium statistical mechanics, where the key dynamical modes are collective'. They provide a central insight:

> ...[T]he genome encodes the information which governs the response of an organism to its physics and biological environment. At the same time, this environment actually shapes genomes through gene transfer processes and phenotype selection. Thus, we encounter a situation where the dynamics must be self-referential: the update rules change during the time evolution of the system, and the way in which they change is a function of the state and thus the history of the system... self-referential dynamics is an inherent and probably defining feature of evolutionary dynamics and thus biological systems.

Again, others have commented on the self-referential character of biological and evolutionary phenomena (e.g., Langton, 1992; Sereno, 1992; Von Neumann, 1966).

Here we explore such self-referential dynamics explicitly from the perspectives of the previous chapters, using the methods of Wallace (2011b). We recognize that the representation of fundamental biological and socioeconomic processes in terms of information sources restrains their inherent nonequilibrium nature. That is, although the operation of information sources is both nonequilibrium and irreversible in the most fundamental sense (e.g., few and short palindromes), the asymptotic limit theorems of information theory beat back, somewhat, the mathematical thicket surrounding such phenomena. The theorems permit something of a formal regularization of inherently nonequilibrium processes under proper circumstances that may lead to the development of new statistical tools for the study of empirical data beyond the narrow confines of network theory.

3.2   Basic formalism

The evolutionary process of generalized Darwinism, in the sense of Aldrich et al. (2008) and Hodgson and Kundsen (2010), as envisioned in the previous chapters, involves dynamic interplay between (at least) three information sources representing transmission of corporate heritage, the cognitive response of a corporation to patterns of threat and opportunity, and embedding environment, given that both corporation and environment 'remember', producing serial correlations in time. We suppose it possible to coarse-grain observational measures of those three processes, representing the results in terms of some 'alphabet' of possible states. Our interest is in (properly characterized, and possibly very long) temporal paths beginning at some initial state a_0, and having the form

$$x_n \equiv \{a_0, a_1, ..., a_n\},$$

where the a_j are possible elements of the coarsegrained alphabet.

Given a particular tripartite starting point, a_0, evolution, being inherently path dependent, must build on what has gone before. Thus, crudely, subsequent paths can be divided into two classes, a vast set having vanishingly small probability, and a much smaller high probability set that, we suppose, follows something like the regularities of information theory that govern the three component information sources. That is, if $N(n)$ is the number of high probability paths of length n, then there exists a *path independent* limit H such that

$$H = \lim_{n \to \infty} \frac{\log[N(n)]}{n}.$$

(3.1)

Below we will indicate how the restriction of path independence might be lifted, somewhat.

We assume that, associated with each path x_n of length n, there is an information source X_n producing it that is defined in terms of the joint and conditional probabilities

$$P(a_0, a_1, ...a_n)$$

and

$$P(a_n|a_{n-1}, ..., a_1, a_0),$$

such that appropriate Shannon uncertainties may be defined (e.g., Ash, 1990; Khinchin, 1957; Cover and Thomas, 2006), and that the Shannon-McMillan Theorem holds:

$$H = \lim_{n \to \infty} \frac{\log[N(n)]}{n} =$$

$$\lim_{n \to \infty} H(X_n | X_{n-1}, ..., X_0) =$$

$$\lim_{n \to \infty} \frac{H(X_0, X_1, ..., X_n)}{n+1}.$$

(3.2)

We now shift perspective, defining equivalence classes of paths, and an associated symmetry groupoid (simplest example, a disjoint union of groups) that will be needed for the characterization of collective phenomena, much in the sense that a symmetry group is needed for Landau's theory of phase transition. See the Chapter Appendix for summary material on groupoids. More detailed treatments can be found in Weinstein (1996) and Brown (1987).

We call two states a_j and a_k equivalent if there is a high probability path beginning with a_0 that reaches them. The set of high probability paths beginning at a_0 defines the possible evolutionary processes that start at that state, and the set of equivalence classes defines a groupoid in a standard manner that characterizes the information source H associated with them.

We can now index the set of possible evolutionary information sources by the groupoids defining the equivalence classes of high probability paths associated with them.

Next, allow the initial state to vary, that is, allow different starting points, a_0, across the system. This produces an even larger groupoid that will enable our analysis of certain collective phenomena.

3.3   Phase transitions

As Feynman (2000) argues, based on work by Bennett (1988), information is simply another form of free energy, and the information in a message is quite precisely measured by the free energy needed to erase it. Indeed, Feynman (2000) shows how to construct an (idealized) machine that directly converts the information in a message to work.

But there are subtleties. First, information sources are already inherently irreversible dynamic systems. For example, in spoken or written English, the short sequence ' the ' has much higher probability than its time reversed ' eht '. There is no local reversibility, and adaptation of methods from nonequilibrium statistical mechanics or thermodynamics will not be graced with 'Onsager reciprocal relations'.

Another subtlety is that, in spite of the inherently nonequilibrium dynamic nature of an information source, the asymptotic limit theorems defining information source uncertainty appear to permit 'nonequilibrium equilibria' in a certain sense.

We suppose there to be some monotonic increasing measure of available free energy M, $Q(\kappa M), Q(0) = 0$ where κ is again an appropriate inverse energy scaling constant. We assume that possible generalized Darwinian trajectories are constrained by the availability of resources, so that the probability of an (inherently irreversible and highly dynamic) information source associated with groupoid element G_j, at a fixed $Q(\kappa M)$, is given, in a first approximation, by the standard expression for the Gibbs distribution

$$P[H_{G_j}] = \frac{\exp[-H_{G_j}/Q]}{\sum_i \exp[-H_{G_i}/Q]}.$$

(3.3)

The Gibbs distribution appears to be not really appropriate for systems evolving in an open manner, and we will generalize the treatment somewhat, using an adiabatic approximation in which the dynamics remain 'close enough' to a form in which the mathematical theory can work, adapting standard phase transition formalism for transitions between adiabatic realms. In particular, rather than using exponential terms, one might well use any functional form $f(H_{Gi}, Q)$ such that the sum over i converges.

In essence, however, by adopting an information source perspective on evolutionary process we implicitly incorporate the possibility of 'nonequilibrium equilibria' in the sense of Eldredge and Gould (1972).

As we shall show, the 'E-property' that Khinchin (1957) identifies – the division of paths into high and low probability sets – the limiting relation

$$\lim_{n \to \infty} \frac{\log[N(n)]}{n} = H$$

and its variants for all high probability paths generated by an ergodic
information source, permit imposition of a powerful regularity onto
inherently nonequilibrium evolutionary processes.

The partition function-analog of this strange system is, as usual,
defined as

$$Z_G(Q) = \sum_i \exp[-H_{G_i}/Q].$$

(3.4)

We can now define a highly simplified evolutionary 'groupoid free
energy', F_G, *constructed over the full set of possible evolutionary tra-*
jectories as constrained by available free energy, as

$$\exp[-F_G/Q] \equiv \sum_i \exp[-H_{G_i}/Q],$$

(3.5)

so that

$$F_G(Q) = -Q \log[Z_G(Q)].$$

(3.6)

This is to be taken as a Morse Function, in the sense of the Mathematical Appendix to this chapter. As we shall show below, other
– essentially similar – Morse Functions may perhaps be defined on
this system, having a more 'natural' interpretation from information
theory.

Argument is now by abduction from statistical physics (Landau
and Lifshitz, 2007; Pettini, 2007). The Morse Function F_G is seen as

constrained by free energy availability in a manner that allows application of Landau's theory of punctuated phase transition in terms of groupoid, rather than group, symmetries.

Recall, now, Landau's perspective on phase transition (Pettini, 2007). The essence of his insight was that certain physical phase transitions took place in the context of a significant symmetry change, with one phase being more symmetric than the other. A symmetry is lost in the transition, i.e., spontaneous symmetry breaking. The greatest possible set of symmetries being that of the Hamiltonian describing the energy states. Usually, states accessible at lower temperatures will lack the symmetries available at higher temperatures, so that the lower temperature state is less symmetric, and transitions can be highly punctuated.

Here, we have characterized the dependence of evolutionary process on the availability of metabolic free energy in terms of groupoid, rather than group, symmetries, and the argument by abduction is essentially similar: Increasing availability of free energy – rising $Q(\kappa M)$ – will allow richer interactions between the three basic economic information sources, and will do so in a highly punctuated manner, as in Eldredge and Gould (1972).

3.4 Extending the model

3.4.1 Kadanoff theory

Given F_G as a free energy analog, we are interested in a mathematical treatment of transitions between adiabatic realms and suppose it possible to define a characteristic 'length', say r, on the system, as more fully described below. We can then define renormalization symmetries in terms of the 'clumping' transformation, so that, for clumps of size R, in an external 'field' of strength J (that we can set to 0 in the limit), one can write, in the usual manner (e.g., Wilson, 1971)

$$F_G[Q(R), J(R)] = f(R)F_G[Q(1), J(1)],$$

$$\chi(Q(R), J(R)) = \frac{\chi(Q(1), J(1))}{R},$$

(3.7)

where χ is a characteristic correlation length.

As Wallace (2005) shows, following Wilson (1971), very many 'biological' renormalizations, $f(R)$, are possible that lead to a number of quite different universality classes for phase transition. Wallace (2005) and Wallace and Fullilove (2008) describe how 'universality class tuning' can be used as a tool for large-scale regulation of the system. See the Mathematical Appendix to this chapter for a summary.

In order to define the metric r, we impose a topology on the system, so that, near a particular 'language' A defining some H_G there is (in an appropriate sense) an open set U of closely similar languages $\hat{A}$, such that $A, \hat{A} \subset U$.

Since the information sources are 'similar', for all pairs of languages $A, \hat{A}$ in U, it is possible to:

1. Create an embedding alphabet which includes all symbols allowed to both of them.

2. Define an information-theoretic distortion measure in that extended, joint alphabet between any high probability (grammatical and syntactical) paths in A and $\hat{A}$, which we write as $d(Ax, \hat{A}x)$ (Cover and Thomas, 2006). Note that these languages do not interact, in this approximation.

3. Define a metric on U, for example,

$$r(A, \hat{A}) = |\lim \frac{\int_{A,\hat{A}} d(Ax, \hat{A}x)}{\int_{A,A} d(Ax, A\hat{x})} - 1|,$$

(3.8)

using an appropriate integration limit argument over the high probability paths. Note that the integration in the denominator is over different paths within A itself, while in the numerator it is between different paths in A and $\hat{A}$. Consideration suggests r is indeed a formal metric.

Clearly, other approaches to metric construction on U seem possible, and other approaches to renormalization than outlined by equation (3.7).

3.4.2   Nonergodic information sources

The ergodic nature of an information source is a generalization of the law of large numbers and implies that the long-time averages can be closely approximated by averages across the probability spaces of those sources. For non-ergodic information sources, a function, $\mathcal{J}(x_n)$, of each path $x_n \to x$, may be defined, such that $\lim_{n \to \infty} \mathcal{J}(x_n) = \mathcal{J}(x)$, but $\mathcal{J}$ will not in general be given by the simple cross-sectional laws-of-large numbers analogs above (Khinchin, 1957).

Let $s \equiv d(x, \hat{x})$ for high probability paths x and $\hat{x}$, where d is a distortion measure, as described in Cover and Thomas (2006). For 'nearly' ergodic systems one might use something of the form

$$ \mathcal{J}(\hat{x}) \approx \mathcal{J}(x) + s d\mathcal{J}/ds|_{s=0} $$

for s sufficiently small. The idea is to take a distortion measure as a kind of Finsler metric, imposing a resulting 'global' structure over an appropriate class of non-ergodic information sources. One question obviously revolves around what properties are metric-independent, in much the same manner as the Rate Distortion Theorem.

These heuristics can be made more precise:

Take a set of 'high probability' paths $x_n \to x$.

Suppose, for all such x, there is an open set, U, containing x, on which the following conditions hold:

1. For all paths $\hat{x}_n \to \hat{x} \in U$, a distortion measure $s_n \equiv d_U(x_n, \hat{x}_n)$ exists.

2. For each path $x_n \to x$ in U there exists a pathwise invariant function $\mathcal{J}(x_n) \to \mathcal{J}(x)$, in the sense of Khinchin (1957, p.72). While such a function will almost always exist, only in the case of an ergodic information source can it be identified as an 'entropy' in the usual sense.

3. A function $F_U(s_n, n) \equiv f_n \to f$ exists, for example,

$$ f_n = s_n, \log[s_n]/n, s_n/n, $$

and so on.

4. The limit

$$ \lim_{n \to \infty} \frac{\mathcal{J}(x_n) - \mathcal{J}(\hat{x}_n)}{f_n} \equiv \nabla_F \mathcal{J}|_x $$

exists and is finite.

Under such conditions, standard global atlas/manifold constructions are possible. Again, $\mathcal{J}$ is not simply given by the usual expressions for source uncertainty if the source is not ergodic, and the phase transition development above may be correspondingly more complicated. Restriction to high probability paths simplifies matters considerably, although precisely characterizing them may be difficult, requiring extension of the Shannon-McMillan Theorem and its Rate Distortion generalization.

An essential question is under what circumstances this differential treatment for 'almost' ergodic information sources permits something very much like what Khinchin (1957, p. 54) calls the 'E property' enabling classification of paths into a small set of high probability and a vastly larger set of vanishingly small probability (Khinchin, 1957, p. 74).

3.4.3 Network theory

As Goldenfeld (2010) has pointed out, equation (3.3), the Gibbs distribution, seems, on the surface, not really appropriate for a system evolving in an open manner, although, as we have argued, the regularities imposed by the asymptotic limit theorems of information theory permit study of 'nonequilibrium equilibria' in a standard way via the interpretation of equation (3.6) as a Morse Function. For example, the Gibbs distribution approach has had considerable success in reframing key results in protein folding dynamics (Wallace, 2010b). Here we extend that treatment, adopting a perspective from network information theory (e.g., Cover and Thomas, 2006; El Gamal and Kim, 2010). The theory is, however, much a work in progress, with many unsolved difficulties. As El Gamal and Kim note, the simplistic model of a network consisting of separate links and naive forwarding nodes does not capture many important aspects of real world networked systems that involve multiple sources with various messaging requirements, redundancies, time and space correlations, and time variations. As they note, the goal in many information systems is not merely to communicate source information, but to make a decision or coordinate an action – in our context, cognitive process. Indeed, the first paper on network information theory was by Claude Shannon himself, who did not solve the question of optimal rates, a matter that remains open (Shannon, 1961), along with many others.

We suppose that a measure of available free energy is itself associated with an information source, Z, representing the intents of an external 'farmer' who provides regulation to the system. This source represents an identifiable subset of the environmental dynamics and provides an embedding context for evolutionary process. It defines jointly typical paths (Cover and Thomas, 2006) for an associated set of economic information sources.

Given three interacting information sources, Y_1, Y_2, Z, the splitting criterion for tripartite jointly typical sequences, taking Z as an external context, is (Cover and Thomas, 2006, p. 524)

$$I(Y_1; Y_2|Z) = H(Z) + H(Y_1|Z) + H(Y_2|Z) - H(Y_1, Y_2, Z),$$

(3.9)

where $H(...|...)$ and $H(...,...,...)$ represent conditional and joint uncertainties (Ash, 1990; Khinchin, 1957; Cover and Thomas, 2006).

This presumably generalizes to something like

$$I(Y_1; ...; Y_n|Z) = H(Z) + \sum_{j=1}^{n} H(Y_j|Z) - H(Y_1, ..., Y_n, Z).$$

(3.10)

Analogous, in a sense, to the 'epigenetic catalysis' arguments of Wallace and Wallace (2009 Sec. 4), the 'farmer' Z creates a directed developmental channel, at the considerable expense of maintaining the Z-structure. That is, a great deal of energy/effort must be put into the regulatory apparatus of the farmer in order to ensure the proper developmental trajectory of the overall system.

Note particularly that, in the absence of an explicit rational farmer, Z represents the effect of the embedding ecosystem, *and the overall structure becomes mutually interacting and fully self-dynamic.*

A subtle question arises at this point regarding the selective value of I in equation (3.10). If information source uncertainty is the splitting criterion of interest, Ash (1990) makes the observation:

> [W]e may regard a portion of text in a particular language as being produced by an information source. The probabilities $P[X_n = a_n|X_0 = a_0, ..., N_{n-1} = a_{n-1}]$ may be estimated from the available data about the language; in this way we can estimate the uncertainty associated with the language. A large uncertainty means, by the [Shannon-McMillan Theorem], a large number of 'meaningful' sequences. Thus given two languages with uncertainties H_1 and H_2 respectively, if $H_1 > H_2$, then in the absence of noise it is easier to communicate in the first language; more can be said in the same amount of time. On the other hand, it will be easier to reconstruct a scrambled portion of text in the second language, since fewer of the possible sequences on length n are meaningful.

Following this argument, in circumstances of high noise we might well find small values of I in equation (3.10) would have greater selective value than larger. Such questions remain to be explored.

More complicated multivariate typical sequences receive much the same treatment (El Gamel and Kim, 2010, p.2-26). Given a basic set of information sources $(X_1, ..., X_k)$ that one partitions into two ordered sets $X(\mathcal{K})$ and $X(\mathcal{K}')$, then the splitting criterion becomes $H(X(\mathcal{K})|X(\mathcal{K}'))$. Generalization to three or more such ordered sets is straightforward.

Then the joint splitting criterion – I, H above – however it may be expressed as a composite of the underlying information sources and their interactions, satisfies a relation closely analogous to the first one in equation (3.2), where $N(n)$ is the number of high probability jointly typical paths of length n. This expression is, then, essentially the same as equations (3.5) and (3.6) in that the joint splitting criterion *is given as a functional composition of the underlying information sources and their interactions*.

There are two immediate implications of this insight.

First, I in equation (3.10) and its generalizations can be considered as Morse Functions in the sense of the Mathematical Appendix that can be parameterized in terms of the monotonic expression involving some appropriate index of available free energy Q. The natural association of equivalence classes of evolutionary states and trajectories with groupoid symmetries then suggests that Landau's spontaneous symmetry breaking arguments, extended to groupoids, will again apply, producing richer and more 'symmetric' socioeconomic processes and structures as Q increases, leading to analogs to serial endosymbiosis and a sequence of 'eukaryotic-like' transitions to more highly structured socioeconomic systems.

Second, since I in equation (3.10) and its generalizations have the form of a free energy, we can *directly* invoke biological-like renormalization relations like equation (3.7) (Wallace, 2005), e.g.,

$$I[Q(R), J(R)] = f(R)I[Q(1), J(1)],$$

$$\chi(Q(R), J(R)) = \frac{\chi(Q(1), J(1))}{R},$$

(3.11)

where we again parameterize by the scalar function Q of available metabolic free energy as above. The splitting criterion I and its generalizations are supposed to be adiabatically piecewise stationary ergodic between phase transitions, so that the asymptotic limit theorems work 'well enough', while the transitions themselves are associated with universality classes according the particular form of $f(R)$. The universality class tuning of Wallace (2005) permits regulation of the phase transitions, and allows another layer of external control.

This reformulation is, then, a more complete answer to concerns regarding the appropriateness of the Gibbs distribution under these circumstances, although characterization of F_G from equation (3.6) as a Morse Function might well be a sufficient argument.

In summary, I in equation (3.10) and the more complicated versions of the splitting criteria for multivariate typical sequences are to be taken as Morse Functions, so that Pettini's (2007) topological hypothesis applies, and Landau's symmetry breaking arguments carry through, albeit in a groupoid context, so that 'symmetry', i.e. evolutionary complexity, can increase with increase in available free energy in an inherently punctuated manner. I and the other splitting criteria analogous to equation (3.10), however, have, in a sense, a more 'natural' interpretation than F_G.

The inference is that choice of a proper Morse Function may depend strongly on context, with a simple Gibbs distribution sufficient for strongly 'physics-bound' processes such as protein folding (Wallace, 2010b), while more complex splitting criteria are to be associated with more complex biological, social, or economic phenomena.

3.4.4   Large deviations reconsidered

Wallace (2010a) has taken a particularly recognizable nonequilibrium statistical mechanics approach to evolutionary dynamics. In that work the interaction of genes, (cognitive) gene expression, and environmental information sources is expressed using the coevolutionary formalism of Chapagnat et al. (2006). The basic idea is to write each information source as a function of those with which it interacts:

$$H_m = H_m(Q_1, ..., Q_s, ...H_j...), j \neq m.$$

where the Q_k represent other relevant parameters. The dynamics of such a system is defined by the usual recursive network of stochastic differential equations, using gradients in a 'disorder' construct as analogs to the more usual gradients in entropy, the thermodynamic forces:

$$S_m \equiv H_m - \sum_j \partial H_m / \partial K_j,$$

(3.12)

where we have expressed both the H_j and Q_j as driving parameters K_j, again with the proviso that one not express H_m directly as a function of itself.

Then, via the homology between information and free energy, the dynamics become driven by the usual Onsager set of stochastic differential equations,

$$dK_t^j = \sum_i [L_{i,j}(t, ..\partial S_m / \partial K_i..)dt + \sigma_{i,j}(t, ..\partial S_m / \partial K_i..)dB_t^i]$$

$$= L_j(t, K_1, .., K_n)dt + \sum_i \sigma_{i,j}(t, K_1, .., K_n)dB_t^i$$

(3.13)

where we have collected and simplified terms. L_j and the $\sigma_{i,j}$ are functions, and the terms dB_t^j represent different kinds of 'noise' constrained by particular forms of quadratic variation, in the usual manner. Standard texts abound.

Again, since information sources are not locally time-reversible, there are no 'Onsager reciprocal relations'.

Reiterating the arguments of Chapter 1, several patterns are obvious.

1. Setting this system of equations to zero and solving for stationary points gives quasi-equilibrium attractor states since the noise terms preclude unstable equilibria. The system then undergoes diffusive drift about the equilibrium configuration.

2. The system may converge to a limit cycle or a pseudorandom strange attractor.

3. What is converged to, however, is not a simple state or set of such states. Rather, this system, via the constraints imposed by the asymptotic limit theorems of information theory, converges to an

equivalence class of of highly dynamic information sources coupled by mutual crosstalk, and equivalence classes define groupoids, as above. In effect, via the Shannon-McMillan Theorem that defines the information source uncertainty, we have driven the mathematical thicket one layer back, expressing a dynamical system in terms of a relatively simple formalism abducted from nonequilibrium statistical mechanics.

As Champagnat et al. (2006) note, however, shifts between the quasi-equilibria of this system of equations can be addressed by the large deviations formalism. They find that the issue of evolutionary dynamics drifting away from trajectories predicted by the canonical equation can be investigated by considering the asymptotic of the probability of 'rare events' for the sample paths of the diffusion.

To reiterate, by 'rare events' they mean diffusion paths drifting far away from the canonical equation. The probability of such rare events is governed by a large deviation principle: when a critical parameter (designated ϵ) goes to zero, the probability that the sample path of the diffusion is close to a given rare path ϕ decreases exponentially to 0 with rate $\mathcal{I}(\phi)$, where the 'rate function' $\mathcal{I}$ can be expressed in terms of the parameters of the diffusion. This result, in their view, can be used to study long-time behavior of the diffusion process when there are multiple attractive evolutionary singularities. Under proper conditions the most likely path followed by the diffusion when exiting a basin of attraction is the one minimizing the rate function $\mathcal{I}$ over all the appropriate trajectories. The time needed to exit the basin is of the order $\exp(V/\epsilon)$ where V is a quasi-potential representing the minimum of the rate function $\mathcal{I}$ over all possible trajectories.

Again, an essential fact of large deviations theory is that the rate function $\mathcal{I}$ which Champagnat et al. invoke can almost always be expressed as a kind of entropy, that is, having the canonical form

$$\mathcal{I} = -\sum_j P_j \log(P_j)$$

(3.14)

for some probability distribution. As indicated, this result goes under a number of names; Sanov's Theorem, Cramer's Theorem, the Gartner-Ellis Theorem, the Shannon-McMillan Theorem, and so forth (Dembo and Zeitouni, 1998; R. Wallace and R.G. Wallace, 2008). A more complete treatment of large deviations theory is provided in the chapter's Mathematical Appendix.

These considerations lead very much in the direction of equation (3.13), but now seen as subject to internally-driven large deviations *that are themselves described as information sources*, providing H-parameters that can trigger punctuated shifts between quasi-stable modes, in addition to resilience transitions driven by 'catastrophic' external events or the exchange of heritage information between different classes of 'organisms', in a large sense.

Figure 3.1 is a schematic that links this perspective to the Morse Theory treatment of section 3.4.3. I, as a Morse Function, is subject to punctuated transitions in a driving 'metabolic' parameter that we call Q. As Q increases, for example, spontaneous symmetry breaking permits, say, a transition to more complex 'eukaryotic' structures via some analog to serial endosymbiosis: the transition from the lower cluster to the higher. But this is seen to take place via a highly structured large deviation *that is itself constrained as being the output of an information source*. This may be determined by internal self-dynamic forces, or it may be imposed from without by a culturally-specific 'farmer'. Decrease in Q can result in punctuated structural collapse.

The spontaneous symmetry breaking argument is thereby seen as a simplified approximation to the coevolutionary formalism of Champagnat et al. (2006), as adapted by Wallace (2010a). Such transitions can occur, but, unlike simple physical systems, need not occur, in the absence of a large deviation that is itself highly structured. To reiterate, in figure 3.1, change of available indices of free energy (or other resources) is a necessary, but not sufficient, condition for punctuated evolutionary change that must be driven by a 'self-dynamic' or 'farmed' large deviation having either its own grammar and syntax or that given it by the farmer.

3.4.5   Stochastic differential geometry

The model of equation (3.13) can be reexpressed using the formalism of equation (3.8).

We have not made explicit the parameters K_j, and can incorporate them into $r(A, \hat{A})$ to produce a simple-appearing stochastic Onsager equation of the form

$$dr/dt = L dS/dr + \sigma W(t),$$

(3.15)

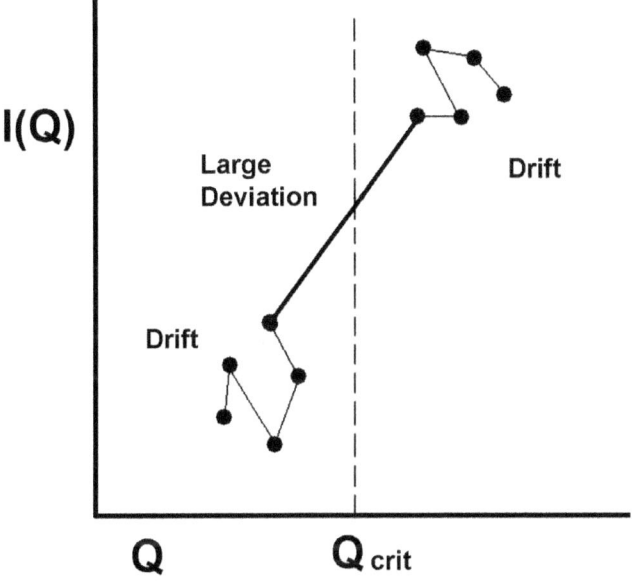

Figure 3.1: Spontaneous symmetry breaking in I as an approximation to a structured large deviation driven by change in a monotonic index of available free energy. Unlike a simple physical system, such a transition can occur if Q increases/decreases beyond Q_{crit}, but will not do so in the absence of a highly structured large deviation. Change in Q is therefore a necessary, but not sufficient, condition. In a 'farmed' system the large deviation is directed by the intent of the farmers. In a 'creative destruction' Schumpeterian system, the large deviation is entirely determined by self-referential internal phenomena, independent of the wishes or welfare of those who constitute the individual elements of that system.

representing the dynamics of the 'flow' from A to $\hat{A}$, where L and σ are constants and $W(t)$ represents noise. This generalizes to the stochastic differential equation

$$dr_t = L(t,r)dt + \sigma(t,r)dB_t,$$

(3.16)

where L and σ are appropriately regular functions of t and r and dB_t represents the noise structure, characterized by its quadratic variation.

This 'simplification', however, leads directly to deep realms of stochastic differential geometry, in the sense of Emery (1989), most easily seen by reintroducing an explicit parameterization for $r(A, \hat{A})$.

Letting the parameters be a vector $\mathbf{K}$ having components K_j, we assume it is possible to write $r(A, \hat{A})$ in terms of a metric tensor $g_{i,j}(\mathbf{K})$ as

$$r(A, \hat{A}) = \int_A^{\hat{A}} [\sum_{i,j} g_{i,j}(\mathbf{K}) \frac{dK_i}{dt} \frac{dK_j}{dt}]^{1/2} dt,$$

(3.17)

where the integral is taken over some parameterized curve from A to $\hat{A}$. Substituting this result into the two equations above produces very complicated expressions in the parameters K_j. Some simplification is possible using a standard hand-waving argument. Various semi-plausible resource-limitation considerations suggest that a minimal $r(A, \hat{A})$ will be more probable than one using more 'energy'. Application of the calculus of variations to minimize equation (3.17) produces a classical geodesic equation having the traditional component-by-component form

$$d^2 K_i/dt^2 + \sum_{j,m} \Gamma^i_{j,m} \frac{dK_j}{dt} \frac{dK_m}{dt} = 0,$$

(3.18)

where the Γ terms are the famous Christoffel symbols involving sums and products of $g_{i,j}$ and $\partial g_{i,j}/\partial K_m$. This must be extended by the introduction of noise $W(t)$ in terms of dB_t to produce Emery's stochastic differential geometry. Although we do not explore the development further, it is clear that this formalism provides a 'highly natural' means of introducing complications such as geographic structure in the underlying populations of interest, albeit only in a necessary conditions regression model-like format that provides limiting riverbanks for, but does not otherwise determine, the flow of a self-dynamic evolutionary process.

3.5 Regulation by information catalysis

Incorporating the influence of a regulatory context – the 'epigenetic' effects of the farmer – can be viewed from another perspective by invoking the Joint Asymptotic Equipartition Theorem (JAEPT) (Cover and Thomas, 2006). For example, given an embedding contextual information source, the influence, Y, of the farming entity, that affects system development, then the dual cognitive source uncertainty of the firm, for example, say H_{D_i}, is replaced by a joint uncertainty $H(X_{D_i}, Y)$. The objects of interest then become the jointly typical dual sequences $z^n = (x^n, y^n)$, where x is associated with the cognitive functioning of the firm and y with the embedding contextual regulating agent or agency. Restricting consideration of x and y to those sequences that are in fact jointly typical allows use of the information transmitted from Y to X as the splitting criterion.

One important inference is that, from the information theory 'chain rule' (Cover and Thomas, 2006),

$$H(X,Y) = H(X) + H(Y|X) \leq H(X) + H(Y),$$

while there are approximately $\exp[nH(X)]$ typical X sequences, and $\exp[nH(Z)]$ typical Z sequences, and hence

$$\exp[n(H(X) + H(Y))]$$

independent joint sequences, there are only about

$$\exp[nH(X,Y)] \leq \exp[n(H(X) + H(Y))]$$

jointly typical sequences, so that the effect of the embedding regulatory context, in this model, is to lower the *relative* free energy of a particular developmental channel for the firm.

Extending the argument by induction to larger scales, the effect of the epigenetic regulation of the farmer is to channel development of the overall system into pathways that might otherwise be inhibited by an energy barrier, in a broad sense. Hence the epigenetic information source Y acts as a *tunable catalyst*, a kind of second order cognitive enzyme, to enable and direct developmental pathways at various scales. This result permits hierarchical models in a natural way.

It critical to note that this is analogous to a relative energy argument, since, metabolically, two systems must now be supported, i.e., that of the 'farmed' economy itself, and that of its catalytic regulator. 'Programming' and stabilizing inevitably intertwined, as it were.

West-Eberhard (2003) argues, in a purely biological context, that any new input, whether it comes from the genome, like a mutation, or from the external environment, like a temperature change, a pathogen, or a parental opinion, has a developmental effect only if the preexisting phenotype is responsive to it. A new input causes a reorganization of the phenotype, or 'developmental recombination'. In developmental recombination, phenotypic traits are expressed in new or distinctive combinations during ontogeny, or undergo correlated quantitative change in dimensions. Developmental recombination can result in evolutionary divergence at all levels of organization.

Individual development can be visualized as a series of branching pathways. Each branch point, according to West-Eberhard, is a developmental decision, or switch point, governed by some regulatory apparatus, and each switch point defines a modular trait. Developmental recombination implies the origin or deletion of a branch and a new or lost modular trait. It is important to realize that the novel regulatory response and the novel trait originate simultaneously. Their origins are, in fact, inseparable events. There cannot, West-Eberhard concludes, be a change in the phenotype, a novel phenotypic state, without an altered developmental pathway.

These mechanisms, at the level of the firm, are accomplished in our formulation by allowing the set B_1 in section 1.4 to span a distribution of possible 'final' states. Then the associated groupoid arguments of Chapter 2 expand to permit traverse of both initial states and possible final sets, recognizing that there can now be a possible overlap in the latter, and the farmer's epigenetic effects are realized through the joint uncertainties $H(X_{D_i}, Y)$, so that the epigenetic information source of the farmer, Y, serves to direct as well the possible final states. Argument by induction to the full hierarchical structure of the economic ecosystem is direct.

These considerations can be made more precise.

Of necessity, $H(X, Y) < H(X) + H(Y)$ if $H(Y|X) < H(Y)$. This implies that, by means of the identification of information as a form of free energy, at the expense of adding the considerable energy burden of the regulatory apparatus, represented by its dual information source Y, it becomes possible to canalize the reaction paths of figure 2.1, so as to make one set of pathways beginning with $\mathbf{S_0}$ far more probable than another.

That is, by raising the entire reaction free energy landscape corresponding to $H(X)$ by the amount $H(Y)$ it becomes possible to deepen the energy channel leading from $\mathbf{S_0}$ to some desired outcome. Complicated internal reaction mechanisms have been subsumed by the Shannon-McMillan Theorem, in the same sense that the Central Limit Theorem subsumes the behavior of long sums of stochastic variates into the Normal distribution.

Within systems of interest, however, there will be ensembles of possible developmental states and pathways, driven by available 'metabolic' free energy, so that, taking $< .. >$ as representing an average,

$$[< H(X,Y) >] < [< H(X) > + < H(Y) >].$$

Typically, letting M represent an index of the intensity of available free energy, a rate measure, one expects

$$< H > \approx \frac{\int H \exp[-H/\kappa M] dH}{\int \exp[-H/\kappa M] dH} \approx \kappa M,$$

where κ, an inverse energy rate scaling constant, may be quite small indeed, a consequence of entropic translation losses between available free energy and the expression of information.

The resulting relation, $M_{X,Y} < M_X + M_Y$, suggests an explicit free energy mechanism for developmental canalization.

If entropic translation losses are not linear with increase in information transmission rate H, we might replace κM with some function $Q(\kappa M)$ that 'tops out' with increasing M, for example $Q \propto \log[\kappa M]$. This means that, after a certain point, large increases in metabolic free energy are needed to increase social or biological information. The energy relation then becomes, after a little algebra,

$$M_{X,Y} < \kappa \times M_X \times M_Y \ll M_X + M_Y,$$

if either κ or one of the other M-terms is small, and a low energy information source regulator could thus be used to 'leverage' reaction canalization very efficiently.

In reality, there will be a large, nested, set of appropriately coarse-grained regulatory and/or signaling processes expressed as information sources – $Y_1, ..., Y_m$ – in which the systems of interest will be embedded, ranging from sets of 'firms', in the largest sense, to patterns of social and cultural interaction, mediated by historical inheritance. We then obtain the set of relations

$$[< H(X, Y_1, ..., Y_m) >] < [< H(X) > + \sum_j < H(Y_j) >],$$

$$M_{X, Y_1, ..., Y_m} < M_X + \sum_j M_{Y_j},$$

$$M_{X, Y_1, ..., Y_m} < \kappa^m M_X \Pi_j M_{Y_j} \ll M_X + \sum_j M_{Y_j}.$$

That is, quite counterintuitively, entropic loss can be a powerful tool for triggering complex institutional logic gates.

The last expression suggests, in particular, that the appropriate regulatory level for intervention – farming – *may not be that of the desired target*. That is, the model implies that the most efficient intervention may be upstream from the desired target or, more likely, involve synergistic dynamic intrusions at more than one scale or level of organization to bring down the overall magnitude of the product term.

3.6   Evolutionary game dynamics

Evolutionary game theory, by contrast to the approach of this work, is supposed to provide both a necessary and sufficient model for evolutionary process, according the the famous replicator equation of Taylor and Jonker (1978). Here we follow closely the arguments of Roca et al. (2009). Given an evolutionary game with payoff matrix W, the dynamics of the distribution of strategy frequencies, x_i as elements of a vector $\mathbf{x}$, is determined by the relation

$$dx_i/dt = x_i[(W\mathbf{x})_i - \mathbf{x}^T W \mathbf{x}].$$

(3.19)

where the term $\mathbf{x}^T W \mathbf{x}$ ensures that $\sum x_i = 1$. Dynamical systems theory then derives the consequences, noting that an appropriate change of variables converts this equation into a system of the Lotka-Volterra type.

Several assumptions are implicit to this perspective:

1. The population is infinitely large.

2. Individuals meet randomly or play against each other, such that the payoff strategy is proportional to the payoff averaged over the current population state.

3. There are no mutations, so that strategies increase or decrease in frequency only due to reproduction.

4. The variation of the population is linear in the payoff difference. Roca et al. (2009) find the approach seriously lacking:

> Evolutionary game dynamics is one of the most fruitful frameworks for studying evolution in different disciplines, from Biology to Economics. Within this context, the approach of choice for many researchers is the so-called replicator equation, that describes mathematically the idea that those individuals performing better have more offspring and thus their frequency in the population grows. While very many interesting results have been obtained with this equation in the three decades elapsed since it was first proposed, it is important to realize the limits of its applicability. One particularly relevant issue in this respect is that of non-mean-field effect, that may arise from temporal fluctuations or from spatial correlations, both neglected in the replicator equation... [T]hese temporal and spatial effects [introduce] non-trivial modifications... when compared to the outcome of replicator dynamics [as do questions of nonlinearity]...

The necessary conditions, regression model-like, dynamic approach we have introduced here can incorporate both spatial structure and temporal fluctuation in a natural manner, although at the evident expense of assumptions of sufficiency.

3.7 Escaping the howling wilderness

The self-referential nature of generalized Darwinian evolutionary process is truly remarkable. While dependent on indices of available free energy and constrained by physical principles and historical trajectory, raw evolution is a language that speaks itself. For example, available free energy, written as $Q(\kappa M)$ above, can itself be an evolutionary product, as, in biological systems, with the aerobic transition. In socioeconomic terms, the acquisition of fire, domestication of farm animals for plowing, development of road systems enabling transfer, hence increased availability of existing energy and resources, development of steam technology, use of fossil fuels, and so on, provide examples. The formal description of such bootstrapping will require more comprehensive methods than are available by abduction from relatively simple physical theory.

Again, the example of figure 3.1 suggests that changes of indices representing available free energy can be a necessary, but not sufficient, condition for eukaryotic-like transitions to greater complexity, or, inversely for structural collapse.

Firms instantiate cognitive processes that take cues from the embedding environment to produce behavioral responses via an analog to the epigenetic catalysis of Wallace and Wallace (2009). Modes of such expression having adaptive value can become fixed in the cultural heritage of the firm by learning or selection: systems requiring too much 'energy' for phenotypic adaptation to environmental demands will fail. Such evolutionary dynamics in simple Schumpeterian market economies will remain self-dynamic, self-referential, continually bootstrapping phenomena. In effect, Schumpeterian economies are languages that speak themselves, independent of the needs or wishes of those embedded in them.

But a socioeconomic system, unlike possible biological counterparts, is a cultural artifact. There is nothing 'natural' to any particular such construct, although the dynamics are constrained by resource availability in the context of historical trajectory and other cultural factors. Within those riverbanks the socioeconomic stream can flow according to its own dynamics, or it can be subject to rigorous cultural channeling. The metaphors of hunter-gatherer vs. farmer are not inappropriate.

Farmed ecosystems are inherently more productive, from a human perspective, than what can be gathered from raw nature. The transition from literal hunter-gatherer societies to neolithic farming enabled the subsequent construction of rich human ecosystems, including cities, city-states, and more elaborate structures. At present, Western ideologies of unregulated 'free markets' have given unfettered reign to an enormous structure with self-dynamic 'large deviations' that possess a grammar and syntax whose internal logic is unaffected by human needs or concerns. Some billions of us ride a rampant, rapidly evolving, socioeconomic engine that has neither engineer nor conductor. We are, very essentially, a tribe of primitive hunter-gatherers at the mercy of an unstable ecological monstrosity that we do not have the political will to control. Emerging from the present howling wilderness of neoliberal capitalism will require a farmed economic ecosystem, a large-scale 'agricultural' economics that must be culturally tailored to local conditions. As with language, music, art, and all the rest, there can be no one, fixed farmed economy that will fit all needs at all times.

The universality class tuning outlined in the Mathematical Appendix to this chapter provides some insight into means of regulating otherwise disruptive phase transitions in economic systems.

There is, of course, a cautionary note to what we have done here. Pielou (1977, p. 106) warns that mathematical models in biology and ecology are only useful as subordinate partners in a continuing dialog with data: models can only recommend perspectives for subsequent empirical test that, in turn, can be used to correct the models. Replacing the intellectual straightjacket of one set of economic theories with another driven by the asymptotic limit theorems of information theory will not address the essential scientific problems now facing generalized evolutionary theory applied to economic process. These will yield only to data-based empirical study in which mathematical models are only one among many possible tools: the word is not the thing.

3.8 Mathematical appendix

3.8.1 Morse Theory

Morse theory examines relations between analytic behavior of a function – the location and character of its critical points – and the underlying topology of the manifold on which the function is defined. We are interested in a number of such functions, for example a 'free energy' constructed from information source uncertainties on a parameter space and 'second order' iterations involving parameter manifolds determining critical behavior. These can be reformulated from a Morse theory perspective. Here we follow closely the elegant treatments of Pettini (2007).

The essential idea of Morse theory is to examine an n-dimensional manifold M as decomposed into level sets of some function $f : M \to \mathbf{R}$ where $\mathbf{R}$ is the set of real numbers. The a-level set of f is defined as

$$f^{-1}(a) = \{x \in M : f(x) = a\},$$

the set of all points in M with $f(x) = a$. If M is compact, then the whole manifold can be decomposed into such slices in a canonical fashion between two limits, defined by the minimum and maximum of f on M. Let the part of M below a be defined as

$$M_a = f^{-1}(-\infty, a] = \{x \in M : f(x) \le a\}.$$

These sets describe the whole manifold as a varies between the minimum and maximum of f.

Morse functions are defined as a particular set of smooth functions $f : M \to \mathbf{R}$ as follows. Suppose a function f has a critical point x_c, so that the derivative $df(x_c) = 0$, with critical value $f(x_c)$. Then f is a Morse function if its critical points are nondegenerate in the sense that the Hessian matrix of second derivatives at x_c, whose elements, in terms of local coordinates are

$$H_{i,j} = \partial^2 f / \partial x^i \partial x^j,$$

has rank n, which means that it has only nonzero eigenvalues, so that there are no lines or surfaces of critical points and, ultimately, critical points are isolated.

The index of the critical point is the number of negative eigenvalues of H at x_c.

A level set $f^{-1}(a)$ of f is called a critical level if a is a critical value of f, that is, if there is at least one critical point $x_c \in f^{-1}(a)$.

Again following Pettini (2007), the essential results of Morse theory are:

1. If an interval $[a, b]$ contains no critical values of f, then the topology of $f^{-1}[a, v]$ does not change for any $v \in (a, b]$. Importantly, the result is valid even if f is not a Morse function, but only a smooth function.

2. If the interval $[a, b]$ contains critical values, the topology of $f^{-1}[a, v]$ changes in a manner determined by the properties of the matrix H at the critical points.

3. If $f : M \to \mathbf{R}$ is a Morse function, the set of all the critical points of f is a discrete subset of M, i.e. critical points are isolated. This is Sard's Theorem.

4. If $f : M \to \mathbf{R}$ is a Morse function, with M compact, then on a finite interval $[a, b] \subset \mathbf{R}$, there is only a finite number of critical points p of f such that $f(p) \in [a, b]$. The set of critical values of f is a discrete set of $\mathbf{R}$.

5. For any differentiable manifold M, the set of Morse functions on M is an open dense set in the set of real functions of M of differentiability class r for $0 \le r \le \infty$.

6. Some topological invariants of M, that is, quantities that are the same for all the manifolds that have the same topology as M, can be estimated and sometimes computed exactly once all the critical points of f are known: Let the Morse numbers $\mu_i(i = 1, ..., m)$ of a function f on M be the number of critical points of f of index i, (the number of negative eigenvalues of H). The Euler characteristic of the complicated manifold M can be expressed as the alternating sum of the Morse numbers of any Morse function on M,

$$\chi = \sum_{i=0}^{m} (-1)^i \mu_i.$$

The Euler characteristic reduces, in the case of a simple polyhedron, to

$$\chi = V - E + F$$

where V, E, and F are the numbers of vertices, edges, and faces in the polyhedron.

7. Another important theorem states that, if the interval $[a, b]$ contains a critical value of f with a single critical point x_c, then the topology of the set M_b defined above differs from that of M_a in a way which is determined by the index, i, of the critical point. Then M_b is homeomorphic to the manifold obtained from attaching to M_a an i-handle, i.e., the direct product of an i-disk and an $(m - i)$-disk.

Again, Pettini (2007) contains both mathematical details and further references. See, for example, Matusmoto (2002) or the classic by Milnor (1963).

3.8.2   Universality class tuning

Biological renormalization

Equation (3.7) states that the information source and the correlation length, the degree of coherence on the underlying network, scale under renormalization clustering in chunks of size R as

$$H[K_R, J_R]/f(R) = H[J, K]$$

$$\chi[K_R, J_R]R = \chi(K, J),$$

with $f(1) = 1, K_1 = K, J_1 = J$, where we have slightly rearranged terms.

Differentiating these two equations with respect to R, so that the right hand sides are zero, and solving for dK_R/dR and dJ_R/dR gives, after some consolidation, expressions of the form

$$dK_R/dR = u_1 d\log(f)/dR + u_2/R$$

$$dJ_R/dR = v_1 J_R d\log(f)/dR + \frac{v_2}{R} J_R.$$

(3.20)

The $u_i, v_i, i = 1, 2$ are functions of K_R, J_R, but not explicitly of R itself.

We expand these equations about the critical value $K_R = K_C$ and about $J_R = 0$, obtaining

$$dK_R/dR = (K_R - K_C)yd\log(f)/dR + (K_R - K_C)z/R$$

$$dJ_R/dR = wJ_Rd\log(f)/dR + xJ_R/R.$$

(3.21)

The terms $y = du_1/dK_R|_{K_R=K_C}, z = du_2/dK_R|_{K_R=K_C}, w = v_1(K_C, 0), x = v_2(K_C, 0)$ are constants.

Solving the first of these equations gives

$$K_R = K_C + (K - K_C)R^z f(R)^y,$$

(3.22)

again remembering that $K_1 = K, J_1 = J, f(1) = 1$.

Wilson's (1971) essential trick is to iterate on this relation, which is supposed to converge rapidly near the critical point, assuming that for K_R near K_C, we have

$$K_C/2 \approx K_C + (K - K_C)R^z f(R)^y.$$

(3.23)

We iterate in two steps, first solving this for $f(R)$ in terms of known values, and then solving for R, finding a value R_C that we then substitute into the first of equations (3.7) to obtain an expression for $H[K, 0]$ in terms of known functions and parameter values.

The first step gives the general result

$$f(R_C) \approx \frac{[K_C/(K_C - K)]^{1/y}}{2^{1/y} R_C^{z/y}}.$$

(3.24)

Solving this for R_C and substituting into the first expression of equation (3.7) gives, as a first iteration of a far more general procedure (Shirkov and Kovalev, 2001), the result

$$H[K, 0] \approx \frac{H[K_C/2, 0]}{f(R_C)} = \frac{H_0}{f(R_C)}$$

$$\chi(K, 0) \approx \chi(K_C/2, 0) R_C = \chi_0 R_C,$$

(3.25)

which are the essential relationships.

Note that a power law of the form $f(R) = R^m, m = 3$, which is the direct physical analog, may not be biologically reasonable, since it says that 'language richness' can grow very rapidly as a function of increased network size. Such rapid growth is simply not observed.

Taking the biologically realistic example of non-integral 'fractal' exponential growth,

$$f(R) = R^\delta,$$

(3.26)

where $\delta > 0$ is a real number which may be quite small, equation we can be solve for R_C, obtaining

$$R_C = \frac{[K_C/(K_C - K)]^{[1/(\delta y + z)]}}{2^{1/(\delta y + z)}}$$

(3.27)

for K near K_C. Note that, for a given value of y, one might characterize the relation $\alpha \equiv \delta y + z = $ constant as a 'tunable universality class relation' in the sense of Albert and Barabasi (2002).

Substituting this value for R_C back gives a complex expression for H, having three parameters: δ, y, z.

A more biologically interesting choice for $f(R)$ is a logarithmic curve that 'tops out', for example

$$f(R) = m \log(R) + 1.$$

(3.28)

Again $f(1) = 1$.

Using Mathematica 4.2 or above to solve equation (3.24) for R_C gives

$$R_C = [\frac{Q}{LambertW[Q\exp(z/my)]}]^{y/z},$$

(3.29)

where

$$Q \equiv (z/my)2^{-1/y}[K_C/(K_C - K)]^{1/y}.$$

The transcendental function LambertW(x) is defined by the relation

$$LambertW(x)\exp(LambertW(x)) = x.$$

It arises in the theory of random networks and in renormalization strategies for quantum field theories.

An asymptotic relation for $f(R)$ would be of particular biological interest, implying that 'language richness' increases to a limiting value with population growth. Taking

$$f(R) = \exp[m(R-1)/R]$$

(3.30)

gives a system which begins at 1 when $R = 1$, and approaches the asymptotic limit $\exp(m)$ as $R \to \infty$. Mathematica 4.2 finds

$$R_C = \frac{my/z}{LambertW[A]},$$

(3.31)

where

$$A \equiv (my/z)\exp(my/z)[2^{1/y}[K_C/(K_C - K)]^{-1/y}]^{y/z}.$$

These developments indicate the possibility of taking the theory significantly beyond arguments by abduction from simple physical models, although the notorious difficulty of implementing information theory existence arguments will undoubtedly persist.

Universality class distribution

Physical systems undergoing phase transition usually have relatively pure renormalization properties, with quite different systems clumped into the same 'universality class,' having fixed exponents at transition (Binney et al., 1986). Biological and social phenomena may be far more complicated:

If the system of interest is a mix of subgroups with different values of some significant renormalization parameter m in the expression for $f(R, m)$, according to a distribution $\rho(m)$, then the first expression in equation (3.7) should generalize, at least to first order, as

$$H[K_R, J_R] =< f(R, m) > H[K, J]$$

$$\equiv H[K, J] \int f(R, m)\rho(m)dm.$$

(3.32)

If $f(R) = 1 + m\log(R)$ then, given any distribution for m,

$$< f(R) >= 1 + < m > \log(R)$$

(3.33)

where $< m >$ is simply the mean of m over that distribution.

Other forms of $f(R)$ having more complicated dependencies on the distributed parameter or parameters, like the power law R^δ, do not produce such a simple result. Taking $\rho(\delta)$ as a normal distribution, for example, gives

$$< R^\delta >= R^{<\delta>} \exp[(1/2)(\log(R^\sigma))^2],$$

(3.34)

where σ^2 is the distribution variance. The renormalization properties of this function can be determined from equation (3.24), and the calculation is left to the reader as an exercise, and can be done in Mathematica 4.2 or above.

Thus the information dynamic phase transition properties of mixed systems will not in general be simply related to those of a single subcomponent, a matter of possible empirical importance: If sets of relevant parameters defining renormalization universality classes are indeed distributed, experiments observing pure phase changes may be very difficult. Tuning among different possible renormalization strategies in response to external signals would result in even greater ambiguity in recognizing and classifying information dynamic phase transitions.

Important aspects of mechanism may be reflected in the combination of renormalization properties and the details of their distribution across subsystems.

In sum, real biological, social, or interacting biopsychosocial systems are likely to have very rich patterns of phase transition which may not display the simplistic, indeed, literally elemental, purity familiar to physicists. Overall mechanisms will, however, still remain significantly constrained by the theory, in the general sense of probability limit theorems.

Punctuated universality class tuning

The next step is to iterate the general argument onto the process of phase transition itself, producing a tunable punctuation.

As described above, an essential character of physical systems subject to phase transition is that they belong to particular 'universality classes'. Again, this means that the exponents of power laws describing behavior at phase transition will be the same for large groups of markedly different systems, with 'natural' aggregations representing fundamental class properties (Binney et al., 1986).

It appears that biological or social systems undergoing phase transition analogs need not be constrained to such classes, and that 'universality class tuning', meaning the strategic alteration of parameters characterizing the renormalization properties of punctuation, might well be possible. Here we focus on the tuning of parameters within a single, given, renormalization relation. Clearly, however, wholesale shifts of renormalization properties must ultimately be considered as well.

Universality class tuning has been observed in models of 'real world' networks. As Albert and Barabasi (2002) put it,

> The inseparability of the topology and dynamics of evolving networks is shown by the fact that [the exponents defining universality class] are related by [a] scaling relation..., underlying the fact that a network's assembly uniquely determines its topology. However, in no case are these exponents unique. They can be tuned continuously...

Suppose that a structured external environment, itself an appropriately regular information source **Y**, 'engages' a modifiable system characterized by an information source. The environment begins to write an image of itself on the system in a distorted manner permitting definition of a mutual information $I[K]$ splitting criterion according to the Rate Distortion or Joint Asymptotic Equipartition Theorems. K is an inverse coupling parameter between system and environment. At punctuation – near some critical point K_C – the systems begin to interact very strongly indeed, and, near K_C, using a simple physical model,

$$I[K] \approx I_0 [\frac{K_C - K}{K_C}]^\alpha.$$

For a physical system α is fixed, determined by the underlying 'universality class.' Here we will allow α to vary, and, in the section below, to itself respond explicitly to imposed signals.

Normalizing K_C and I_0 to 1,

$$I[K] \approx (1 - K)^\alpha.$$

(3.35)

The horizontal line $I[K] = 1$ corresponds to $\alpha = 0$, while $\alpha = 1$ gives a declining straight line with unit slope which passes through 0 at $K = 1$. Consideration shows there are progressively sharper transitions between the necessary zero value at $K = 1$ and the values defined by this relation for $0 < K, \alpha < 1$. The rapidly rising slope of transition with declining α is of considerable significance:

The *instability* associated with the splitting criterion $I[K]$ is defined by

$$Q[K] \equiv -K dI[K]/dK = \alpha K (1 - K)^{\alpha - 1},$$

(3.36)

and is singular at $K = K_C = 1$ for $0 < \alpha < 1$. Following earlier work (e.g., Wallace and Fullilove, 2008), we interpret this to mean that values of $0 < \alpha \ll 1$ are highly unlikely for real systems, since $Q[K]$, in this model, represents a kind of barrier for 'social' information systems.

On the other hand, smaller values of α mean that the system is far more efficient at responding to the adaptive demands imposed by the embedding structured environment or regulatory authority, since the mutual information which tracks the matching of internal response to external demands, $I[K]$, rises more and more quickly toward the maximum for smaller and smaller α as the inverse coupling parameter K declines below $K_C = 1$. That is, systems able to attain smaller α are more responsive to external signals than those characterized by larger values, in this model, but smaller values will be harder to reach, probably only at some considerable physiological or opportunity cost. Focused conscious action takes resources, of one form or another.

The more biologically realistic renormalization strategies given above produce sets of several parameters defining the universality class, whose tuning gives behavior much like that of α in this simple example.

Formal iteration of the phase transition argument on this calculation gives a tunable regulation, focusing on paths of universality class parameters:

Suppose the renormalization properties of an information source at some 'time' k are characterized by a set of appropriately coarse-grained parameters $A_k \equiv \alpha_1^k, ..., \alpha_m^k$. Fixed parameter values define a particular universality class for the renormalization. We suppose that, over a sequence of 'times', the universality class properties can be characterized by a path $x_n = A_0, A_1, ..., A_{n-1}$ having significant serial correlations which, in fact, permit definition of *another* adiabatically piecewise stationary ergodic information source associated with the paths x_n. Call that source **X**.

Suppose also, in the now-usual manner, that the set of external (or internal, systemic) signals impinging on the information source of basic interest is also highly structured and forms another information source **Y** that interacts not only with the system of interest globally, but specifically with its universality class properties as characterized by **X**. **Y** is necessarily associated with a set of paths y_n.

Pair the two sets of paths into a joint path, $z_n \equiv (x_n, y_y)$ and invoke an inverse coupling parameter, K, between the information sources and their paths. This leads, by the arguments above, to phase transition punctuation of $I[K]$, the mutual information between **X** and **Y**, under either the Joint Asymptotic Equipartition Theorem or under limitation by a distortion measure, through the Rate Distortion Theorem. The essential point is that $I[K]$ is a splitting criterion under these theorems, and thus partakes of the homology with free energy density which we have invoked above.

Activation of universality class tuning, the mean field model's version of attentional focusing, then becomes itself a punctuated event in response to increasing linkage between the organism and an external structured signal or some particular system of internal events.

This iterated argument exactly parallels the extension of the General Linear Model to the Hierarchical Linear Model in regression theory.

Another path to the fluctuating dynamic threshold might be through a second order iteration similar to that just above, but focused on the parameters defining the universality class distributions given above.

3.8.3   The large deviations formalism

It is of some interest to more explicitly carry through the program suggested by Campagnat et al. (2006) via a recapitulation of large deviations and fluctuation formalism.

Information source uncertainty, according to the Shannon-McMillan Theorem, serves as a splitting criterion between high and low probability sequences (or pairs of them) and displays the fundamental characteristic of a growing body of work in applied probability often termed the Large Deviations Program, (LDP). This seeks to unite information theory, statistical mechanics, and the theory of fluctuations under a single umbrella.

Following Dembo and Zeitouni, (1998, p.2), let $X_1, X_2, ...X_n$ be a sequence of independent, standard Normal, real-valued random variables and let

$$S_n = \frac{1}{n} \sum_{j=1}^{n} X_j.$$

(3.37)

Since S_n is again a Normal random variable with zero mean and variance $1/n$, for all $\delta > 0$

$$\lim_{n \to \infty} P(|S_n| \geq \delta) = 0,$$

(3.38)

where P is the probability that the absolute value of S_n is greater or equal to δ. Some manipulation, however, gives

$$P(|S_n| \geq \delta) = 1 - \frac{1}{\sqrt{2\pi}} \int_{-\delta\sqrt{n}}^{\delta\sqrt{n}} \exp(-x^2/2)dx,$$

(3.39)

so that

$$\lim_{n\to\infty} \frac{\log P(|S_n| \geq \delta)}{n} = -\delta^2/2$$

(3.40)

This can be rewritten for large n as

$$P(|S_n| \geq \delta) \approx \exp(-n\delta^2/2).$$

(3.41)

That is, for large n, the probability of a large deviation in S_n follows something much like the asymptotic equipartition relation of the Shannon-McMillan Theorem, so that meaningful paths of length n all have approximately the same probability $P(n) \propto \exp(-nH[\mathbf{X}])$.

Questions about meaningful paths appear suddenly as formally isomorphic to the central argument of the LDP which encompasses statistical mechanics, fluctuation theory, and information theory into a single structure (Dembo and Zeitouni, 1998).

Again, the cardinal tenet of large deviation theory is that the rate function $-\delta^2/2$ can, under proper circumstances, be expressed as a mathematical entropy having the standard form

$$-\sum_{k} p_k \log p_k,$$

(3.42)

for some set of probabilities p_k.

Next we briefly recapitulate part of the standard treatment of large fluctuations (e.g., Onsager and Machlup, 1953; Fredlin and Wentzell, 1998).

The macroscopic behavior of a complicated physical system in time is assumed to be described by the phenomenological Onsager relations giving large-scale fluxes as

$$\sum_{i} C_{i,j} dK_j/dt = \partial S/\partial K_i,$$

(3.43)

where the $C_{i,j}$ are appropriate constants, S is the system entropy, and the K_i are the generalized coordinates which parametize the system's free energy.

Entropy is defined from free energy F by a Legendre transform – more of which follows below:

$$S \equiv F - \sum_{j} K_j \partial F/\partial K_j,$$

where the K_j are appropriate system parameters.

Neglecting volume problems for the moment, free energy can be defined from the system's partition function Z as

$$F(K) = \log[Z(K)].$$

The partition function Z, in turn, is defined from the system Hamiltonian – defining the energy states – as

$$Z(K) = \sum_{j} \exp[-KE_j],$$

where K is an inverse temperature or other parameter and the E_j are the energy states.

Inverting the Onsager relations gives

$$dK_i/dt = \sum_j L_{i,j}\partial S/\partial K_j = L_i(K_1, ..., K_m, t) \equiv L_i(K, t).$$

(3.44)

The terms $\partial S/\partial K_i$ are macroscopic driving forces dependent on the entropy gradient.

Let a white Brownian noise $\epsilon(t)$ perturb the system, so that

$$dK_i/dt = \sum_j L_{i,j}\partial S/\partial K_j + \epsilon(t)$$

$$= L_i(K, t) + \epsilon(t),$$

(3.45)

where the time averages of ϵ are $< \epsilon(t) >= 0$ and $< \epsilon(t)\epsilon(0) >= D\delta(t)$. $\delta(t)$ is the Dirac delta function, and we take K as a vector in the K_i.

Following Luchinsky (1997), if the probability that the system starts at some initial macroscopic parameter state K_0 at time $t = 0$ and gets to the state $K(t)$ at time t is $P(K, t)$, then a somewhat subtle development (e.g., Feller, 1971) gives the forward Fokker-Planck equation for P:

$$\partial P(K, t)/\partial t = -\nabla \cdot (L(K, t)P(K, t)) + (D/2)\nabla^2 P(K, t).$$

(3.46)

In the limit of weak noise intensity this can be solved using the WKB (i.e., the eikonal) approximation, as follows. Take

$$P(K,t) = z(K,t)\exp(-s(K,t)/D).$$

(3.47)

$z(K,t)$ is a prefactor and $s(K,t)$ is a classical action satisfying the Hamilton-Jacobi equation, which can be solved by integrating the Hamiltonian equations of motion. The equation reexpresses $P(K,t)$ in the usual parametized negative exponential format.

Let $p \equiv \nabla s$. Substituting and collecting terms of similar order in D gives

$$dK/dt = p + L,$$

$$dp/dt = -\partial L/\partial K p$$

(3.48)

and

$$-\partial s/\partial t \equiv h(K,p,t) = pL(K,t) + \frac{p^2}{2},$$

(3.49)

with $h(K,t)$ the Hamiltonian for appropriate boundary conditions.

Again following Luchinsky (1997), these Hamiltonian equations have two different types of solution, depending on p. For $p = 0, dK/dt = L(K,t)$, describing the system in the absence of noise. We expect that with finite noise intensity the system will give rise to a distribution about this deterministic path. Solutions for which $p \neq 0$ correspond to *optimal paths* along which the system will move with overwhelming probability.

These results can, however, again be directly derived as a special case of a Large Deviation Principle based on generalized entropies mathematically similar to Shannon's uncertainty from information theory, bypassing the Hamiltonian formulation entirely.

3.8.4 Groupoids

Following Weinstein (1996), states a_j, a_k in a set A are related by the groupoid morphism if and only if there exists a high-probability grammatical path connecting them to the same base point, and tuning across the various possible ways in which that can happen parameterizes the set of equivalence relations and creates the groupoid. This assertion requires some development.

Note that not all possible pairs of states (a_j, a_k) can be connected by such a morphism, that is, by a high-probability, grammatical and syntactical path linking them with some given base point. Those that can define the groupoid element, a morphism $g = (a_j, a_k)$ having the natural inverse $g^{-1} = (a_k, a_j)$. Given such a pairing, it is possible to define 'natural' end-point maps $\alpha(g) = a_j, \beta(g) = a_k$ from the set of morphisms G into A, and a formally associative product in the groupoid $g_1 g_2$ provided $\alpha(g_1 g_2) = \alpha(g_1), \beta(g_1 g_2) = \beta(g_2)$, and $\beta(g_1) = \alpha(g_2)$. Then the product is defined, and associative, $(g_1 g_2) g_3 = g_1 (g_2 g_3)$.

In addition, there are natural left and right identity elements λ_g, ρ_g such that $\lambda_g g = g = g \rho_g$ (Weinstein, 1996).

An orbit of the groupoid G over A is an equivalence class for the relation $a_j \sim G a_k$ if and only if there is a groupoid element g with $\alpha(g) = a_j$ and $\beta(g) = a_k$. Following Cannas da Silva and Weinstein (1999), we note that a groupoid is called transitive if it has just one orbit. The transitive groupoids are the building blocks of groupoids in that there is a natural decomposition of the base space of a general groupoid into orbits. Over each orbit there is a transitive groupoid, and the disjoint union of these transitive groupoids is the original groupoid. Conversely, the disjoint union of groupoids is itself a groupoid.

The isotropy group of $a \in X$ consists of those g in G with $\alpha(g) = a = \beta(g)$. These groups prove fundamental to classifying groupoids.

If G is any groupoid over A, the map $(\alpha, \beta) : G \to A \times A$ is a morphism from G to the pair groupoid of A. The image of (α, β) is the orbit equivalence relation $\sim G$, and the functional kernel is the union of the isotropy groups. If $f : X \to Y$ is a function, then the kernel of f, $ker(f) = [(x_1, x_2) \in X \times X : f(x_1) = f(x_2)]$ defines an equivalence relation.

Groupoids may have additional structure. As Weinstein (1996) explains, a groupoid G is a topological groupoid over a base space X if G and X are topological spaces and α, β and multiplication are continuous maps. A criticism sometimes applied to groupoid theory is that their classification up to isomorphism is nothing other than the classification of equivalence relations via the orbit equivalence relation and groups via the isotropy groups. The imposition of a compatible topological structure produces a nontrivial interaction between the two structures. Below we will introduce a metric structure on manifolds of related information sources, producing such interaction.

In essence, a groupoid is a category in which all morphisms have an inverse, here defined in terms of connection to a base point by a meaningful path of an information source dual to a cognitive process.

As Weinstein (1996) points out, the morphism (α, β) suggests another way of looking at groupoids. A groupoid over A identifies not only which elements of A are equivalent to one another (isomorphic), but *it also parameterizes the different ways (isomorphisms) in which two elements can be equivalent*, i.e., all possible information sources dual to some cognitive process. Given the information theoretic characterization of cognition presented above, this produces a full modular cognitive network in a highly natural manner.

Brown (1987) describes the fundamental structure as follows:

> A groupoid should be thought of as a group with many objects, or with many identities... A groupoid with one object is essentially just a group. So the notion of groupoid is an extension of that of groups. It gives an additional convenience, flexibility and range of applications...
>
> EXAMPLE 1. A disjoint union [of groups] $G = \cup_\lambda G_\lambda, \lambda \in \Lambda$, is a groupoid: the product ab is defined if and only if a, b belong to the same G_λ, and ab is then just the product in the group G_λ. There is an identity 1_λ for each $\lambda \in \Lambda$. The maps α, β coincide and map G_λ to λ, $\lambda \in \Lambda$.
>
> EXAMPLE 2. An equivalence relation R on [a set] X becomes a groupoid with $\alpha, \beta : R \to X$ the two projections, and product $(x, y)(y, z) = (x, z)$ whenever $(x, y), (y, z) \in R$. There is an identity, namely (x, x), for each $x \in X$...

Weinstein (1996) makes the following fundamental point:

> Almost every interesting equivalence relation on a space B arises in a natural way as the orbit equivalence relation of some groupoid G over B. Instead of dealing directly with the orbit space B/G as an object in the category S_{map} of sets and mappings, one should consider instead the groupoid G itself as an object in the category G_{htp} of groupoids and homotopy classes of morphisms.

The groupoid approach has become quite popular in the study of networks of coupled dynamical systems which can be defined by differential equation models, (Golubitsky and Stewart, 2006).

3.9 Acknowledgments

The author thanks Dr. D.N. Wallace for basic insights from population, community, and ecosystem ecology regarding the impossibility of a 'one size fits all' economic system.

3.10 References

Albert, R., A Barabasi, 2002, Statistical mechanics of complex networks, Reviews of Modern Physics, 74:47-97.

Aldrich, H., G. Hodgson, D. Hull, T. Knudsen, J. Mokyr, V. Vanberg, 2008, In defense of generalized Darwinism. Journal of Evolutionary Economics, 18:577-596.

Ash, R., 1990, Information Theory, Dover, New York.

Bennett, C., 1988, Logical depth and physical complexity. In The Universal Turing Machine: A Half-Century Survey. R. Herkin (ed.), pp. 227-257, Oxford University Press.

Binney, J., N. Dowrick, A. Fisher, M. Newman, 1986, The Theory of Critical Phenomena, Clarendon Press, Oxford, UK.

Brown, R., 1987, From groups to groupoids: a brief survey. Bulletin of the London Mathematical Society, 19:113-134.

Caccioli, F., M. Marsilli, P. Vivo, Eroding market stability by proliferation of financial instruments, European Journal of Physics B, 71:467-479.

Cannas Da Silva, A., and A. Weinstein, 1999, Geometric Models for Noncommutative Algebras. American Mathematical Society, Providence, RI.

Cover, T., and J. Thomas, 2006, Elements of Information Theory, Second Edition, John Wiley and Sons, New York.

Champagnat, N., R. Ferriere, and S. Meleard, 2006, Unifying evolutionary dynamics: from individual stochastic process to macroscopic models. Theoretical Population Biology, 69:297-321.

Dembo, A., and O. Zeitouni, 1998, Large Deviations and Applications, Second Edition, Springer, New York.

El Gamal, A., and Y. Kim, 2010, Lecture Notes on Network Information Theory, arXiv:1001.3404v4.

Eldredge, N., and S. Gould, 1972, Punctuated equilibrium: an alternative to pyletic gradualism. In T. Schopf (ed.), Models in Paleobiology, Freeman Cooper and Co., San Francisco.

Emery, M., 1989, Sotchastic Calculus in Manifolds, Springer, New York.

Feller, W., 1971, An Introduction to Probability Theory and its Applications, John Wiley and Sons, New York.

Feynman, R., 2000, Lectures on Computation, Westview Press, New York.

Fredlin, M., A. Wentzell, 1998, Random Perturbations of Dynamical Systems, Springer, New York.

Gabora, L., D. Aerts, 2005, Evolution as a context-driven actualization of potential: Toward an interdisciplinary theory of change of state, Interdisciplinary Science Reviews, 30:69-88.

Gabora, L., D. Aerts, 2007, A cross-disciplinary framework for the description of contextually mediated change, Electronic Journal of Theoretical Physics, 4(15):1-22.

Goldenfeld, N., and C. Woese, 2010, Life is physics: evolution as a collective phenomenon far from equilibrium. ArXiv:1011.4125v1 [q-bio.PE].

Goldenfeld, N., 2010, Personal communication.

Golubitsky, M., and I. Stewart, 2006, Nonlinear dynamics and networks: the groupoid formalism. Bulletin of the American Mathematical Society, 43:305-364.

Haldane, A., R. May, 2011, Systemic risk in banking ecosystems, Nature, 469:351-355.

Hodgson, G., T. Knudsen, 2010, Darwin's Conjecture: The search for general principles of social and economic evolution, University of Chicago Press.

Kastner, M., 2006, Phase transitions and configuration space topology. ArXiv cond-mat/0703401.

Khinchin, A., 1957, Mathematical Foundations of Information Theory. Dover, New York.

Landau, L., and L. Lifshitz, 2007, Statistical Physics, Third Edition, Part 1. Elsevier, New York.

Langton, C., 1992, Life at the edge of chaos. In Artificial Life II, eds. Langton, C., C. Taylor, J. Farmer, S. Rasmussen, Addison-Wesley, Reading, MA.

Luchinsky, D., On the nature of large fluctuations in equilibrium systems: observations of an optimal force, Journal of Physics A, 30:L577-L583.

Matsumoto, Y., 2002, An Introduction to Morse Theory. Translations of Mathematical Monographs, Vol. 208, American Mathematical Society.

Milnor, J., 1963, Morse Theory. Annals of Mathematical Studies, Vol. 51, Princeton University Press.

Odling-Smee, F., K. Laland, and M. Feldman, 2003, Niche Construction: The Neglected Process in Evolution. Princeton University Press, Princeton, NJ.

Onsager, L., S. Machlup, 1953, Fluctuations and irreversible processes, Physical Review, 91:1505-1512.

Pettini, M., 2007, Geometry and Topology in Hamiltonian Dynamics and Statistical Mechanics. Springer, New York.

Pielou, E., 1977, Mathematical Ecology. John Wiley and Sons, New York.

Roca, C., J. Cuesta, A. Sanchez, 2009, Evolutionary game theory: temporal and spatial effects beyond replicator dyanmics, Physics of Life Reviews, 6:208-249.

Sereno, M., 1991, Four analogies between biological and cultural/linguistic evolution, Journal of Theoretical Biology, 151:467-507.

Shannon, C., 1961, Two-way communication channels, in Proceedings of the 4th Berkeley Symposium in Mathematical Statistics and Proability, Vol. 1, University of California Press, pp. 611-644.

Taylor, P., L. Jonker, 1978, Evolutionarily stable strategies and game dynamics, Mathematical Biosciences, 40:145-156.

Von Neumann, J., 1966, Theory of Self-Reproducing Automata, University of Illinois Press.

Wallace, R., and D. Wallace, 2009, Code, context, and epigenetic catalysis in gene expression. Transactions on Computational Systems Biology XI, LNBI 5750: 283-334.

Wallace, R., 2005, Consciousness: A Mathematical Treatment of the Global Neuronal Workspace Model. Springer, New York.

Wallace, R., 2009, Metabolic constraints on the eukaryotic transition. Origins of Life and Evolution of Biospheres, 38:165-176.

Wallace, R., 2010a, Expanding the modern synthesis. Comptes Rendus Biologies, 333:701-709.

Wallace, R., 2010b, Structure and dynamics of the 'protein folding code' inferred using Tlusty's topological rate distortion approach. In press, BioSystems, doi:10.1016/j.biosystems.2010.09.007.

Weinstein, A., 1996, Groupoids: unifying internal and external symmetry. Notices of the American Mathematical Association, 43:744-752.

West-Eberhard, M., 2003, Developmental Plasticity and Evolution, Oxford University Press, New York.

Wilson, K., 1971, Renormalization group and critical phenomena. I. Renormalization group and the Kadanoff scaling picture. Physical Review B, 4:3174-3183.

Index

www.ingramcontent.com/pod-product-compliance
Lightning Source LLC
Chambersburg PA
CBHW051337170526
45166CB00002B/852